I0058092

Video Growth Hacking

for Channel Chiefs

Simple strategies to help your channel partners achieve double-digit growth

Robert Cassard

Business Success Press

Video Growth Hacking for Channel Chiefs

Copyright © 2016 Business Success Press / Robert J.W. Cassard

Published by:

Business Success Press
Berkeley, California
www.BusinessSuccessPress.com

First Edition: May 2016

ALL RIGHTS RESERVED.
No part of this book may be reproduced or transmitted in any form or by any means, including but not limited to information storage retrieval systems, electronic, mechanical, photocopy, recording, etc. without written permission from the copyright holder, except for the inclusion of brief quotations in a review.

Limit of Liability/Disclaimer of Warranty:
While the publisher and author have used their best efforts in preparing this book, they make no representations or warranties with respect to the accuracies or completeness of the contents of this book and specifically disclaim any implied warranties of merchantability or fitness for a particular purpose. No warranty may be created or extended by sales representatives or written sales materials. The advice and strategies contained herein may not be suitable for your situation. The publisher is not engaged in rendering professional services, and you should consult with a professional where appropriate. Neither the publisher nor the author shall be liable for any loss of profit or other commercial damages, including but not limited to special, incidental, consequential or other damages.

ISBN: 978-0-6927-1538-3

Original book format by Derek Murphy @Creativindie
Printed in the United States of America

10 9 8 7 6 5 4 3 2 1

What Channel and Business Leaders are saying...

"Robert is the most creative and talented marketing guru I know. He always sets the bar high, and still he manages to exceed my expectations every time. With this book, he's created an indispensable tool for channel marketers and sales leaders."

Randy Albert, University of Michigan, Ross School of Business
Author of **Making the Transition from Entrepreneurship to Enterprise**

"During my 20+ years as a channel leader at Panasonic *and* MicroAge, *I could really have used the information shared in this book. Cassard's video growth hacking tips may start a channel marketing revolution."*

Sheila O'Neil, VP Channel Strategy, Channel Maven Consulting

"I worked with Robert Cassard and Voodoo on a pair video projects that produced net ROI of 670%. I was amazed how an executive like me could appear on camera once, and the resulting video essentially cloned me — educating, informing and generating demand."

Tim Donahue, Regional President, Sprint

"Robert Cassard 'gets' the channel, both from a vendor and a reseller perspective. Every channel executive would be smart to read this book and apply its advice to their sales and marketing challenges."

Joe Ward, Vice President US Channels, ShoreTel

"Robert and Voodoo have coached our marketing team to use video more effectively and create demand for our channel partners. Their depth of knowledge never ceases to impress me."

Ty Tobin, Supplier Business Executive, Avnet Technology Solutions

"Robert packs a huge amount of valuable information into this little book. Don't be surprised if you walk away with radical new ideas for growing your channel business and gaining job security, too."

Renato Mariani, SVP Marketing & Business Intelligence
Cable & Wireless Communications

"Video is a hot topic in digital marketing for the tech channel. Robert Cassard's book explains everything channel marketers at vendor and distributor companies need to know about automated video."

Michael Bui, Sr. Manager / Channel & Distribution Marketing, Intel Security

"The Mitel-Voodoo partnership has been responsible for millions in net new sales. The eVideo Launcher *is a low-cost alternative to full marketing automation systems and puts video marketing in the hands of small partners on a budget."*

Rich McBee, CEO, Mitel

"Robert has the magic touch for communicating big ideas. His videos and growth hacking strategies have helped sell millions for tech companies and their channel partners. I'm confident this book will help channel leaders take action to change their businesses and their lives."

Allison Maslan, CEO, AMI Global Business Mentoring
Author of **Blast Off! The Surefire Success Plan to Launch Your Dreams into Reality**

"Video has become essential for companies at every level. Robert Cassard is one of the top video consultants in San Francisco."

Andrew Romans, Rubicon Venture Capital
Author of **The Entrepreneurial Bible to Venture Capital**

CONTENTS

Section 2

A roadmap with GPS: high-growth vehicles with turn-by-turn directions... 41

Section 3

Automated video: faster routes to faster growth 71

Section 4

Proven video strategies: turning your roadmap into a flight plan 97

Dedication

To my extraordinary life partner Bara, for her deep insights, boundless empathy, Taurean determination and unconditional love; and to my children Dylan, Elijah and Avalon — each of you is a wonderful gift to our family and the world.

And to my visionary and patient partners and team members at *Voodoo Viral Marketing Systems*. I'm proud to be part of a crack team of hard-working innovators.

Acknowledgements

This book grew from a seed planted by business coach Giles Fabris. He urged me to share the knowledge that was locked up in my head and put it on paper to help transform the lives of Channel Chiefs. It couldn't have been written without the foresight, courage and creativity of the many technology vendors, distributors and channel partners whose products and services Voodoo has helped promote over the past decade. Their creative content and Automated Video Communications programs have yielded the real-world experiences, remarkable successes and reams of data upon which this book is built.

A big shout out to our many friends and colleagues at these technology vendors, distys and channel partners — forgive me if I left anyone out: *10D Tech, 303 Technologies, A-1 Voice & Data, Absolute Communications, Accurate Telecom, Accutel Total Solutions, Adept Networks, Adkins Cabling, Adtran, Advanced*

Communications, Advanced Pro-Com, AdvanTel Networks, Advent Telecom, Alcon DTS, Allstream, Allworx, American Telecom, AmeriTel, Amtel IP Systems, Aruba, Ascam Myco, ATC Telecom, ATSnexgen, Avant Communications, Avaya, Avigilon, Avnet, Axiom Telephone Services, Benbria, Benecom Technologies, BizVoIP, Black Box, Blue Violet Networks, BluePrint Technologies, BoxMeta, Bridgman Communications, Brookside Technology Partners, BSB Communications, BT Mack Enterprises, BTI Communications, Business Electronics Inc., Business Phones Direct, Cady Business Technologies, CBS Telephone and Data, CCC Technologies, CCPlus Inc., CCT Telecomm, Centerpoint Direct, Central New Mexico Electric Cooperative, Ceres Technology Group, Channel Maven, Charleston Telecommunication Consulting, Chesapeake Communications, ChoiceTel, Cisco, Clear2there, CMC Technology Group, Co-nexus Communication Systems, Comcast, ComDirect, Communication Connection Inc., Communication Network Corporation, CommuniTech Services Inc., Computer Telephone Inc., Connell Communications, Control Communications, Converged Digital Networks, Convergence, Copper State Communications, Couchbase, Crexendo, CSI-Networks Telewood Corp, CXM, Cya, CYA Networks, Cynosure Strategies, DashRemind, Data Plus Communications, Data-Smart Computers, Inc., Dependable Technologies Group, Digital Future, Digital I/O, DNDC Telephone Company, DTEL Telecommunications, E55 Technologies, EarthBend, ET&T, Eck-Mundy Associates, Embrace Cortel, EmFusion Technologies, Energy Unleashed, Enhanced Telecommunications, Enterprise Systems Group, eSquared Communications, Excel Telecom, Executone Systems Co. of Louisiana, Expert Technology Associates, Extenda Communications, Facilities Dynamics, First Telecommunications, Five Star Technology Solutions, Five Star Telecom, Frontier Communications, Frontrunner Network Systems,

Fulton Communications, Geetech, Gibson Teldata, GoGrid, Golden West Technologies, Guinness World Records, Heart Technologies, Heartland Technology Solutions, Hi Country Wire & Telephone, HP, Hewlett-Packard Enterprise, HydeTelecom, Hytec Telephone, ICS, ICS Communications, ICS Telecom, IN Communications, Intel Security Group, Integra Telecom, Interconnect Systems, Interwest Communications Dallas, Introtel, IP Communications, ITS Inc., JEM Communications, Jive Communications, Just Solutions, Inc., KB Technologies, Kelcom Voice & Data Solutions, Level (3), Lifesize, Linehan Communications, Logicalis, Logitech, MainPC Group, Mainway Telecom, Marchese Computer Products, Marco, Inc., Maryland Telephone, Matrix Integration, Maverick Networks, McEnroe Voice & Data, Metropolis, MiCloud Business, MidCo Inc., Midwest Technology Services, Millennium Communications, Milner Voice & Data, Minnesota Telephone Networks, Mitel, Mobius Partners, Montgomery Brothers, Morefield Communications, Morse Communications, NEC, Net Activity, Netcom Consulting, Network South, NextStep Networking, nGenx, NJPA, Nimbo iP, Norcom Solutions, OAISYS, Olympic Telephone, Omni Systems, Panasonic, Panasonic Display Solutions, Partners Technology, Pavelcomm, PeAk Communication Systems, Peninsula Communications & NT, PHD Communications, Phybridge, Plantronics, Polycom, Powernet, Premier Network Solutions, Premysis Technologies, Prime Communications, Prime Telecommunications, Professional Communication Systems, Protel Communications, PSS Communications, Punchdown, Quality Communications, REI Technology, Reliable Technology, Rhode Island Telephone, Sage Technology Group, Sencommunications, ShoreTel, Silent Partner Communications, SimpleCom Telecom, Site Services, SkyGuide, SkySon, Sound Inc., Southeastern Telecommunication Services, Sprint, Standard Tel Networks, Star2Star, Statewide

Communications, Stockhausen Technologies, Stores Online, Summit Partners, SUNCO, Suntel Services, Swrve, synergIT, TCE Company, TCI Telcept, TCI (Telecommunications Concepts Inc.), Tec-Pros, Tech Electronics, Technology Systems, Technowledge Inc., Telbon Communications, Telco Wiz Inc., Telcom Innovations Group, Tele-Solutions, Inc., Telec Inc., Telecom Analysts, TeleManagement Pros, Telenet VoIP, Telexperts, Telist Inc., Toshiba, Towner Communications Systems, Trans-West Network Solutions (TWNS), Travis Voice & Data, Tri-County Communications Cooperative, TSAChoice, Tuck Communications Services, Ultimate Ears, Unified USA, US Signal, US Voice & Data, Utility Telephone, Vertical Communications, VibeVoip, Vidyo, Voice and Network Solutions, Voice Plus Communications, VoicePro, VoIPNetworks, WWDataSystems, WatsonCommunications, Windstream, Windstream - ISG, WiSpots, Inc., Works Computing, WTI Communications, Xarios, XFER Communications, XO Hosted Security. Thank you all!

Special thanks to Voodoo's Tech Advisory Board, the feet on the street who help us understand what to say in our proprietary videos and why; and to Heather Margolis (ultimate *Channel Maven* and new mom) and her team, including super-Channel-Chief Sheila O'Neil and super-communicators McNall Mason and Lexi Strickland.

Thanks to my Voodoo family — co-founder Rick Davis: evolutionary partner and friend, with the uncanny ability to fix and optimize *everything*; Michele Riley: 25-year channel advocate and warm-weather Diamondback with the Midwestern work ethic; Angela Servino: the hidden asset that keeps the customers happy;

William Tang: the great and powerful Oz behind the Voodoo curtain; and Robby Milsap: for the fast ideas and future flow.

To the family that molded my business knowledge — David Cassard, Sr.: who taught his boys young by making us shareholders; Olga Cassard: ever-loving and unconditionally supportive mom; Dave Cassard: CPA and legacy-keeper; and Rick Cassard: attorney, professor and East Bay neighbor.

To my top business influencers — Bara Waters: the wisest strategist I know; Joe Ward: channel sales visionary, for lighting the torch and protecting it in threatening winds; Randy Albert: partner in early entrepreneurial ventures; Bruce Jaffe: 'da brain, 'da insights and 'da alchemy; Michael Gerber: small business visionary; Stuart Wilde: for the warrior's wisdom; Shalamee Campbell: for higher perspective every day; Seth Godin: who *lives* outside the box; James Altucher: for the push to *choose myself*; Mike Koenigs: for the impetus to write *now*; Joe Pulizzi: for giving a name to *Content Marketing* and tirelessly advancing the cause; Hugh Morgan: the Canadude, for marketing mastery and shattering the Cone of Silence; and Allison Maslan: the Pinnacle of inspiration, business coaching and networking.

To the stellar group of Channel Chiefs and channel partners who read drafts of the book, offered important suggestions for improvement, and helped keep it real. And to every other soul I love, respect, and neglected to mention. Next time around!

Robert Cassard
Alameda, California

Foreword

Today's channel partners work with anywhere from 5 to 25 vendors, making channel marketing and sales more complex than ever. As a vendor, marketing "to" and "through" channel partners is difficult but necessary. There's a tendency to bombard partners and joint customers with too much information, too often.

I experienced this first-hand while leading channel programs and channel marketing initiatives for several large IT vendors. Within these vendor organizations, typical channel ecosystem challenges and frustrations exist: *how do we keep products and services top-of-mind with partners while communicating directly with the channel community, analysts, and customers?*

In 2009, when I founded *Channel Maven Consulting*, I knew many vendors needed help to improve their channel sales and marketing programs and drive more sales through their partners. They also needed an ally to help build their channel teams, relieve the burden of multi-level communications and understand their unique businesses and priorities.

Channel program challenges grow bigger each year. It's harder than ever to garner the attention of partners and gain the mindshare of their customers using commonly available tools and systems. It takes *more* to win them over.

Video marketing is the hot topic in channel enablement conversations because video allows Channel Chiefs to accomplish things we've all been talking about for years. Other than face-to-face, there is simply no other tool or medium that communicates as efficiently and effectively as video. It's quick, engaging, and can be absorbed while multi-tasking.

Beware: video only works when it's done right. Channel leaders, even at high-levels, often avoid video marketing because they see it as a black box full of mysteries and unanswered questions. *Video Growth Hacking for Channel Chiefs* opens the black box to expose proven ways to use video for double-digit channel growth.

Robert Cassard offers compelling advice backed by experience — evidence gathered from hundreds of videos and thousands of campaigns and drip marketing programs over the past decade.

This book does a favor for the channel community by exposing the secrets of effective video marketing and sharing a "flight plan" any open-minded Channel Chief can use to become a high flying Video Growth Hacker.

Heather Margolis
CEO — Channel Maven Consulting

Section 1

The channel Chief challenge: driving growth without a roadmap

?

1

The "mobile" life of channel and field marketers

E ver since I co-founded a video automation software company back in 2007, I've been deeply embedded in marketing and sales for technology vendors, distributors and channel partners. Watching Channel Chiefs try to grow demand through partners has been like watching an epic corporate football match.

Channel, Field and Product Marketing experts and sales reps execute their plays, extolling the virtues of technology and business solutions like *security* and *mobility*. In the process, many of these channel leaders experience way too much *in*security and "mobility" in their own careers — horizontal and sometimes *downward* mobility.

I've seen many Channel Chiefs forced to "switch teams" from vendor to vendor and reseller to reseller. Some got "traded" with surprising frequency regardless of their hard work and devotion to the team. Employer loyalty? Job security? What are those?

Many channel leaders experience too much "mobility" in their own careers.

From my position on the sidelines, coaching, communicating and suggesting plays, I've spent a lot of time adding new strategies to the channel marketing playbook — developing simpler, easier, more elegant plays. My primary goal has been to help vendors, distributors and channel teams smash their marketing and sales goals. But there's also been a very personal dimension to this.

My team and I get attached to the people we work with at each vendor or distributor company, so it's important to us to help them outperform projections and gain leverage in their own careers.

Have you looked at your job description lately? My guess is it's full of nebulous revenue generation expectations and lofty but vague performance goals. These remind me of clauses in a pre-nup. They allow your employer complete discretion over if and when they decide it's time for you to "go mobile."

Here are a few choice phrases pulled from real channel marketing and sales job descriptions:

- Lead and manage channel account team to achieve or exceed partner sales goals
- Accountable to achieve channel segment revenue growth objectives, as measured by key performance metrics
- Build and launch engagement marketing campaigns to drive demand for primary and additional wallet share products
- Be a top performer, achieving a strong growth record with key stakeholders
- Execute campaigns to raise awareness and generate demand for our solutions
- Set the tone of channel marketing strategy, with success linked to achieving performance targets
- Drive sales, develop and grow sales relationships, increasing revenue with high tech solution providers
- Develop and implement channel expansion strategy

And my personal favorite:
- Drive double digit year-over-year channel growth

Imagine that: you (one person) are responsible for growing the company's channel by 10% or more each year. With vague, bold and even outlandish expectations like these, the question for every channel marketing and sales leader is: *how can I possibly accomplish that?* But the underlying and more nagging question you have to live with every day is: *how long can I hang onto this job?*

2

Use this book to secure your job and bolster your career

If your director- or executive-level title contains the word Channel, Field, Marketing, Product, Sales, Development, Partner or Dealer, then you're a "Channel Chief" and this book is for you. With a small investment of reading time, you'll learn concrete ways to improve your channel's performance and make yourself more valuable at the place where you work. This will be true, even if your employer expects you to be superhuman and "drive double digit year-over-year channel growth."

Channel Chiefs often feel isolated. Few people understand the complex challenges you face, but I certainly do, and I'm determined to offer real help right here and now. Get ready for bold ideas, new perspectives, counterintuitive successes, and foolproof ways to enable your channel.

This book isn't intended to be an exhaustive study on video marketing, rather a helpful reality-based set of tips, insights and inspirations. Some of you may recognize your own stories within these pages. I've avoided naming names both to protect the innocent and because the *lessons* matter more than the brands involved.

Because my company's video software platform has always been *vendor-agnostic*, I've watched many types of tech vendors push a huge variety of campaigns. The *Voodoo Viral Marketing Systems* team and I have seen every imaginable style of video launched through thousands of one-off campaigns and drip-marketing series, and we've learned a lot about what works and what doesn't. I plan to spill that whole can of beans in this brief book.

We'll explore proven ways to get your channel partners pointed in the same direction, to generate new demand and to sell more than ever before. We'll discover how to pursue and achieve channel growth through Automated Video Communications. As you'll see, these techniques are already proven to produce outstanding channel results — the level of success that can make you indispensable.

That's the power of **Video Growth Hacking**.

3

Where are we and how the heck did we get here?

The longer you've worked with channel partners, the more tools you've seen thrown at them, and the more you've seen each latest-greatest tool touted as The Answer.

Every technology company I know was quick to embrace the potential of cloud marketing for its channel partners and became an early adopter.

Marketing and Sales Channel Chiefs got excited about cloud-based systems because they could fulfill vital partner needs from a distance. They also promised unprecedented reporting and proven Return-On-Investment (ROI).

It was a rosy picture: For the first time ever, all partners would be able to access the same version of the same tool with no need for desktop software. All partners would be able to do the same thing at the same time in the same way. Like magic, all partner marketing and sales activity would be unified and synergistic. And vendor-level channel marketing and sales staff would be able to see and measure it all, with complete visibility into partner usage and results. The campaigns that Marketing worked so hard to develop would finally generate the Sales impact everyone desired. Plus, Channel Chiefs would automatically be able to prove campaign efficacy and, in turn, their value to their own companies and their partners.

In hindsight, that picture looked a little *too* rosy. But why? It seemed pretty easy:
- Do some research and due diligence
- Pick one or two excellent SaaS tools
- Give them to your partners

Partners would start using them, and success would happen quickly.

But that's not at all what happened. While Channel Chiefs were evaluating tools to recommend, many partners were already excited about choosing *their own* cloud-based systems and software. As usual, most partners went rogue: they did their own research, and they picked and adopted their own tools for Customer Relationship Management (e.g. *Salesforce*), business process management (e.g.

TigerPaw), email marketing (e.g. *Constant Contact*), social media outreach, estimating and quoting, etc.

The spacious, high-speed, limited-access highway of cloud marketing was promising to get us where we needed to go, much faster. But before we knew it, there were way too many vehicles on the road and no lane markings to prevent collisions. Ultimately, vendors and channel partners were faced with a lot *more* options, more complexity, more roadblocks, and a traffic jam of competing platforms that yielded slow or no progress.

As usual, most partners went rogue— they did their own research, and they picked and adopted their own tools.

Every cloud software company hawked their own proprietary roadmap to the promised land. And although every vendor and partner knew where they wanted and intended to go, most of them independently arrived at a destination called Confusion.

Lately, it's felt like ground hog day for many Channel Chiefs: you get back on the road every day, determined to drive your company's marketing and sales with the latest map and directions, hoping to zig-zag your way to marketing and sales Utopia.

4

"Are we there yet?"

L ike a kid bored in the backseat on a long car ride, you're probably wondering why it's taking so long for all these impressive cloud-based marketing vehicles to get you where you originally expected to go. In fact, most Channel Chiefs have started to wonder if they'll *ever* arrive.

From the channel partner perspective, the marketing roadmap is filled with endless detours, construction zones, side-trips and off-ramps. And they have to keep reading their maps **while driving**: running their businesses, closing deals and servicing clients.

Stop a moment and itemize all the ways your company currently enables its channel partners to help them market and sell for you.

How many different tools and systems are in use? Is it even possible to do a quick inventory in your head?

For virtually every tech company my team and I have worked with, we've encountered a partner portal filled with a dizzying array of tools and resources:

- Co-branded (syndicated) websites
- Customizable collateral
- Video libraries with download/embed options
- PR and other prepared content for Social Media posting
- Deal registration and protection
- Sales support
- Product demos
- Pre-sales engineering
- Certification programs
- Configure, Price and Quote (CPQ) tools
- Online customer and order tracking
- Seasonal and time-sensitive promotions (often with partner tier-based variations)
- Incentive and bonus programs (also with partner tier-based variations)

I'm sure I've left out a few. Given all that content and complexity, it's no wonder your channel partners rarely listen when you and your team reach out to help them. They tune out the majority of emails and newsletters. They don't answer your phone calls.

For almost 10 years now, my team has informally surveyed hundreds of channel partners. When we ask about marketing and sales resources provided by vendors through partner portals, partners respond by saying something about how overwhelming it is, usually describing "systems and information overload" or something similar. They appreciate all the things you *try* to do for them; it's usually just too much for them to grapple with. In most cases, they don't have the time or the staff to make sense of it all, let alone to utilize everything you offer to their (and your) maximum advantage.

The all-in-one campaign trend

The desire to simplify and improve channel marketing programs has led to the enablement trend of multi-channel all-in-one campaigns often referred to as campaigns-in-a-box. These theoretically provide partners everything they need to launch fully customized campaigns, all in one "easy-to-use" package.

But easy is relative, and often these multi-channel programs involve a complex mix of email marketing, social media, co-branded landing pages, capture forms, etc. So even this noble attempt at simplifying partners' lives often falls flat and isn't simple at all.

Recently we watched one vendor spend an enormous amount of time and money creating a beautiful set of fully customizable campaigns for their partners. These were good looking, intelligently integrated campaigns. And they were packaged with instructions for use with various common SaaS marketing platforms and tools.

Among the many campaign components the vendor supplied the channel were the following 10 items:

1) **A campaign playbook** explaining when and how to launch the campaign elements
2) **Lead-capture landing page templates** to install on partner websites
3) **Outbound email templates** to open doors and begin conversations with prospects
4) **Telemarketing scripts** to help reps respond to leads and qualify them
5) **Social media messages** to post on LinkedIn, twitter and Facebook to enhance and maintain campaign momentum
6) **A list of resources and links** to help partners during the later stages of the buyer's journey
7) **Tracking recommendations** for campaign results
8) **Strategies for targeting and list segmentation**
9) **Setup instructions** for partners who have a Marketing team
10) **Setup instructions** for partners who **don't** have a Marketing team (using designated 3rd-party assistance)

The Good:
- Professional, all-in-one, creative outbound campaigns.
- Deployment methodology anticipating partner objections and challenges.
- Campaigns co-branded for each partner.

The Bad:
- Far too complicated for most partners to implement.
- Instructions assume most partners use certain tools and platforms, which many do not.
- Self-promotional campaigns, overly focused on the vendor. (Text mentions the vendor name too often and is full of marketing speak.)
- Written as promotional advertisements, not helpful, customer-centered content.
- Campaigns co-branded for each partner, but not personalized from each sales rep.
- Campaigns do not incorporate any video!

The Glorious:
At the time these all-in-one campaigns were introduced, my company, known informally as Voodoo, didn't have a direct relationship with the vendor. However, we worked with a number of the vendor's channel partners, who made us aware of the new program.

We knew multiple partners that were eager to participate and launch the vendor campaigns, but weeks later, they were still struggling to get everything set up.

As we watched partners attempt to cobble together multiple systems to launch the diverse campaign elements, we saw an opportunity to help. We took the following actions:
- Imported the graphics, email templates and custom-branded landing pages into their Voodoo accounts.

- Modified the content to focus on prospects' needs, not the vendor's brand.
- Created multi-stage drip campaign options for more consistent outreach and better results.
- Added video click-through elements to enhance engagement.
- Added rep-level personalization to improve response.
- Connected the email templates to lead capture and tracking mechanisms to provide real-time action alerts to sales reps.

The purpose of this integrated approach was to enable turn-key deployment of the vendor's multi-channel campaigns, allowing participating partners to login to a single account, choose a campaign and contact list and launch.

Using a unified tool, these partners were able to launch any campaign from the vendor series in less than 5 minutes. The campaigns immediately began generating new leads, while literally hundreds of other partners were still trying to set things up or had simply given up.

5

Who are you: Channel Marketer, Sales Chief or Growth Hacker?

E arlier, we explored what your vendor-employer expects you to accomplish and the nearly impossible demands your work is often measured against.

Seth Godin has written a compelling book on this topic called *Linchpin: Are You Indispensable?* He explains that linchpin employees are the essential building blocks of a great organization. They may not be famous but they're indispensable, which usually gains them the best jobs and the most freedom. Godin says, "Every day I meet people who have so much to give but have been bullied enough or frightened enough to hold it back. It's time to stop complying with the system and draw your own map. You have brilliance in you, your contribution is essential, and the art you create is precious. Only you can do it, and you must."

I like that Godin uses the word 'art' to describe each employee's unique contribution because Marketing is an art and so is Sales. Depending on your title, you probably identify your role mostly as one or the other, but your accountability goals probably fall in the shared area of the Venn diagram *between* the two.

Marketers generally don't succeed without an excellent Sales process and team and sales reps don't succeed without excellent marketing tools and support. The intersecting area of Marketing and Sales is what the C-Suite REALLY really wants you and your counterparts to deliver, and it boils down to one word: **Growth.**

If you can devise a way to grow partner sales faster, the folks in the C-Suite will love you, give you raises and do almost anything to keep you. In other words, what your vendor-employer really wants and needs, without knowing how to articulate it, is for you to be a **growth hacker**.

The origin of the growth hacker

The term growth hacker was coined by tech investor Sean Ellis back in 2010, when he was at *Air BNB*. He was describing a hybrid kind of marketer-coder he'd witnessed becoming vital to start-up companies. So-called growth hackers were focused on using creative, low-cost and often non-traditional marketing techniques to build their user base. As Ellis describes it, "A growth hacker is a person whose true north is growth."

Growth hacking has been highly valued by startups, but larger organizations are catching on because they can derive such massive benefit from it. Becoming a growth hacker takes both imagination and moxie, and is the direction in which all marketing is inevitably moving, especially in the tech sector and especially for online marketing and sales.

What is growth hacking?
Excerpted and paraphrased from Wikipedia:

Growth hacking is a marketing technique which aims to attract users at a relatively low cost and primarily by means of technological integration. It focuses on lowering cost per customer acquisition, facilitating word-of-mouth advertising and increasing customer lifetime value.

Growth hackers generally focus on low-cost alternatives to traditional marketing, e.g. using social media and viral marketing instead of buying advertising through more traditional media such as radio, newspaper, and television.

Marketers who claim to specialize in growth hacking use various types of classic marketing—persuasive copy, email marketing, SEO and viral strategies, among others, with a purpose to increase conversion rates and achieve rapid growth. It also involves online community management and social media outreach, building a brand's image on social media outlets, and performance metrics to sell products and gain exposure.

Growth hacking can be seen as part of the online marketing ecosystem, since growth hackers use techniques such as search engine optimization, website analytics, content marketing and A/B testing.

Quick clarification: When I talk about growth *hacking*, I'm not talking about anything illegal, nor am I suggesting you need to become a computer programmer to be good at this. Growth hacking in the channel space usually means having the creative courage to be inventive and ingenious about marketing and sales. It means thinking boldly and differently, and *taking action* to harness communication tools and technology to achieve the fastest growth possible.

You'll never help your channel take quantum leaps with the same old tools and tired techniques.

The day I started growth hacking.

My first job out of college was as a Junior Copywriter at a Michigan advertising agency. Just a month or two into the job, I had started writing TV and radio ads for the agency's largest client, a Midwestern "superstore" grocery chain.

When it came time for the client's annual agency review, it was obvious the Account Executive was worried. He needed "fresh ideas" to pitch the client and prove our value, so he asked the creative team to get to work.

The agency's production budgets and media buys had always been limited by client advertising budgets which, in turn, limited our agency's income and profits, too.

Without realizing it, I stopped thinking like a copywriter and started thinking about the true north of growth. I asked myself why this grocery chain had such limited advertising budgets. Was there an easy way to find money to solve that problem?

The agency had been producing a lot of "donut" ads for the client. Each TV and radio ad featured one or more products in the middle, like a donut. I started wondering about the inherent value of those product placements.

A quick conversation with the AE revealed that the store chain was basically giving away product ad placement to vendors to earn their loyalty and maximize the product discounts the store received.

So I asked: what if we could determine a combined "advertising value" or "exposure value" of each product placement? Could we package each placement into a comprehensive, discounted, business-building program for vendors?

The program would request a specific co-op marketing dollar investment from the grocery vendors. In exchange, they'd receive a pre-determined amount of product exposure in the form of Gross Rating Points (GRPs) on TV and radio, column-inches in print ads, AND product placement in end-cap displays at multiple stores, with point-of-sale displays and graphics.

When the AE heard the idea, he lit up and began working with me to refine the concept. By the time we presented the program to the client, it had a name, a logo, and standardized pricing for all vendors. It was a synergistic formula: the vendor would pay $X but would receive ROI of $Y + Z in media exposure and store shelf space and promotion.

This was **win-win-win growth hacking**:
  • **Our agency's revenue soared** as the infusion of new cash

from vendor participants doubled the grocery chain's advertising budget overnight.

- **Vendor sales spiked** from the synergistic promotion program, which prompted more and more vendors to participate.
- **The grocery chain more than doubled its exposure** from media advertising, grew profits, and mounted a rapid expansion with new stores in more states.

As for me, I got a whopping $2,000 annual raise and the word "Junior" dropped from my Copywriter title. Of all the stakeholders involved, I gained the least — by far.

Ultimately, though, I gained three things that became **very** valuable to me:

- the impetus to start my own company
- the confidence to know that one of my simple ideas could result in quantum growth
- a good story to tell in this book

6

The Growth Hacker Mindset

As you might infer from Wikipedia's definition, a growth hacker doesn't replace a marketer or sales leader…at least not yet. But as online marketing sage Neil Patel warns, "[The growth hacker's] absolute focus on growth has given rise to a number of methods, tools, and best practices, that simply didn't exist in the traditional marketing repertoire, and as time passes the chasm between the two disciplines deepens."

Marketers and sales leaders who adopt the growth hacker mindset now are far more likely to achieve the often-unreasonable revenue and growth demands stated in their job descriptions. And their value to an employer will skyrocket as a result. When you think like a growth hacker, every marketing or sales decision you make is informed primarily by its impact on growth, and to a much lesser extent by traditional Key Performance Indicators (KPIs). This means all the initiatives, strategies and tactics you propose will obsessively serve the goal of growth.

This growth obsession works like a physical cleanse. You simplify your KPIs, your goals, and the tools you need to reach them. When you start ignoring everything that doesn't yield growth, you *stop* trying to do everything you've always done and hanging onto all the old tools and hype-laden "content" that by now is probably doing you and your partners more harm than good.

Most importantly, you stop adding items and complexity to your channel marketing programs and portals in the hope of achieving incremental change. Instead, you clean house, replacing the ineffective and outmoded elements of your channel enablement programs in bold pursuit of exponential change through streamlined new approaches.

When you start ignoring everything that doesn't yield growth, you stop trying to do everything you've always done and hanging onto all the old tools...

By mustering up the growth hacker's courage to say *out with the old*, you free up space, you clarify, you simplify. And you open up sales potential in your partners that you never knew existed. They need **simple** (it's all they have time for) and they want **effective**.

Want to get your partners' attention? Tell them you're about to clean out your entire partner portal and get rid of all the old stuff. Ask them what really works and what they insist that you keep or improve. (It may not be much.)

The formula is remarkably straightforward: Start fresh with an easy-to-use, automated toolset and a streamlined body of authentic "help-not-hype" content. Tie your content delivery directly to each stage of The Buyer's Journey and Customer Lifecycle. In other words, make it foolproof for partners to know what content to use, when, and how.

I'll explain how some of your peers are doing this as we continue along our route.

▶

Section 2

A roadmap with GPS: high-growth vehicles with turn-by-turn directions

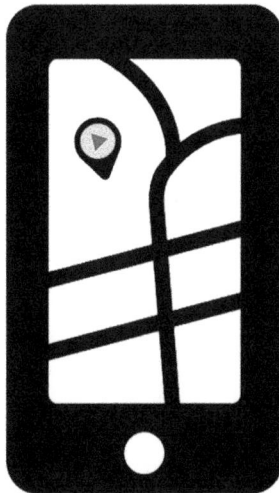

7

Video facts: why partners need strategic video content

Perhaps you're uncertain about escalating automated video to the top of your channel marketing priorities, or you're concerned about convincing your Marcom colleagues to drop much of what they're doing in favor of video. Here are 8 reasons why you and your partners *need* strategic video content more than any other type of marketing vehicle.

1) **Video is *the* marketing trend for fast-growing B2B businesses.** 96% of B2B companies plan to use video marketing in 2016. *(Merchant Marketing Group)*

2) **Video gives your partners a major SEO advantage.** Adding video

to the Home page of a partner's website increases their chance of a front-page Google result by 53X. *(Nate Elliot/Forrester Research)*

3) **Video helps your partners build *rockstar* brands** and grow beyond their local markets. YouTube is now the #2 global search engine. *(YouTube)* That means your partners must be "findable" on YouTube with professional, high-value videos or you'll miss out on a sizable chunk of sales growth.

4) **Video *forces* your partners to grow.** It makes their email marketing almost twice as effective, because an introductory email that includes a video link typically posts a 96% increase in Click-Through-Rate (CTR). *(Implix)* Couple this CTR increase with tracking that notifies partner reps about *who* clicked-through and *when*. Now you have a huge strategic growth advantage.

5) **Video makes each channel partner's social media promotions far more effective.** Instead of the low engagement most partners experience with their blogs or related social posts, their audience is projected to engage 10X more with video content. *(Content Marketing Institute)*

6) **Video builds relationships and earns the trust of potential buyers.** There are a number of reasons why this happens naturally, and some are physiological and some are psychological. For example, the human brain processes visuals 60,000 times faster than text. *(3M Corporation and Zabisco)* And stories are 22x more memorable than facts alone. *(Michelle Clayman, Stanford University)*

And my personal favorite:

7) **Video is sticky.** Viewers recall 95% of what they see in a video, but only 10% of what they read. *(Online Publishers Association)*

Do you still doubt that video is the most important marketing and sales investment you can make and the best growth hack you can provide your partners? Here's one more reason:

8) **Video converts better than *anything else*.** 71% of marketers say conversion rates from video outperform all their other marketing content. *(Vidyard)* Nothing else comes close, and I'll bet most of the remaining 29% haven't tried video yet!

Beyond all the impressive statistics, there are other less measurable but equally potent reasons video is essential to you and your partners:

- Video **engages the audience directly**
- Video **conveys your perfectly crafted message every time**
- Video **makes your brand, solutions and partners real, likeable and trustworthy**, thereby lowering purchase barriers
- Video **leverages time** — you can reach unlimited prospects and customers with messages recorded only once

8

Gaining the emotional advantage

Now you've absorbed the statistics and put yourself in growth hacking mode. As a Channel Chief, your first question is likely to be: *What's the single fastest way to jump-start channel sales and post measurable growth?*

The answer can be summed up in two words: **automated video.** Later, I'll explain in detail what **automated** means, but first, let's examine **video** itself, and figure out why video has become the #1 growth weapon in the channel marketing arsenal.

Video is the proven way to communicate with emotional impact online. Emotion is what sells, convinces, and makes people feel comfortable with and trust you and your brand. Think about how hard it is to inject emotion into written words on a web page. Usually, the more emotion even a brilliant copywriter attempts to convey, the more it feels fake and inauthentic. BS detectors start blinking red, especially the highly tuned BS detectors of the millennial generation, who hate being "sold to." When writers start adding exclamation marks to make their point more emphatically, prospects sense the desperation and pull away, often never to return.

Emotion is what sells, convinces, and makes people feel comfortable with and trust you and your brand.

Strategic and professional video content generally has the opposite effect. A real person on-camera — communicating via the medium of high-quality visuals and sound — can show enthusiasm, and even passion, and people watching simply *know* when it's authentic.

The ability to communicate emotionally and authentically on-demand makes video the most effective way to communicate both *to* and *through* your channel partners. Often, online video can communicate as effectively as being there in person. With the right combination of visuals, words and music, it can be even *more* effective because video viewers are usually on their own turf (in their own home or office), relaxed and with their guard down.

If strategic and authentic video content isn't the cornerstone of your channel marketing and sales enablement programs yet, or if you have a library of some videos, but they look and feel too much like traditional TV advertising and sales hype, then you're missing the emotional advantage of engaging, helpful and valuable video content. This means you're losing business…probably a *lot* of business.

9

The Video Bandwagon:
climb on or get trampled

There's a massive video bandwagon rolling across the internet. It's happening because most buying today occurs through online research, and video is more and more essential to that process. As millennials move into decision-making roles with IT and telecom buying authority, your sales will tank without video to support each stage of their buyer's journey.

In the B2C space, the major online retailers all figured this out a few years ago. Already by the end of 2012, 48 out of the top 50 online retailers were using video to help sell products and increase revenue. *(source: Sunday Sky)*

But when *all* brands, including smaller ones, are taken into account, only 24% are using online video in their marketing. (*Kantar Media*) That's a lot of lost potential.

In the B2B world, video can be a bonanza, particularly for small and emerging businesses trying to stand out (including the majority of your channel partners). It's one way they can be *better* than the big companies they're forced to compete with online. A small to medium-sized channel partner can gain a significant advantage simply by being more personal, more authentic and more helpful.

Channel marketing growth hack: the automated video funnel

As I write this, my company has spent nearly a decade monitoring and amassing the results of thousands of technology video campaigns broadcast from corporate and individual accounts.

We've seen some very ambitious campaigns and drip marketing programs produce embarrassing results. But far more often, we've seen simpler, lower-cost and often more personal campaigns and drip programs generate astounding ROI—paying for themselves tens, or even hundreds, of times over. At this point, the Voodoo team has developed a sixth sense about which approaches are likely to take off and which are likely to flat-line for high-ticket B2B IT and telecom marketing and sales.

If you asked me to sum up all the experience we've gleaned into an all-encompassing video growth hacking methodology, it would be this:

The most effective mechanisms for channel partners to sell a vendor's products and services are *automated video funnels*. These marketing systems consist of ongoing targeted outreach (through personal, emotional, truthful, and value-giving video messages and written messages), aimed at the primary growth goals of sales conversion, customer satisfaction and referral generation.

Compared to your and your partners' other marketing options, automated video funnels cost less, provide better and more predictable results and virtually guarantee high (often *ridiculously* high) return on your Marketing Development Funds (MDF) investment.

Case study: How one tech manufacturer migrated from inside sales to channel sales using automated video

My company has developed channel enablement programs for major tech companies including some of the most successful Unified Communications & Collaboration (UCC) manufacturer-vendors.

Most UCC vendors sell through hundreds of channel partners of all types and sizes. Sometimes, the vendors also have an added distributor layer between their channel marketing and sales team and certain partners. Getting all these partners to communicate with equal professionalism and consistency can be like an episode of **Mission: Impossible.**

In one case, we'd worked with the vendor for about three years, and the value of automated video had proven itself at an impressive scale with remarkable consistency. The inside sales team had been using video to educate prospects and customers about their solutions, and the company's own CRM and closed/won data confirmed ROI in the hundreds of percent month after month. (The very first month of reported data showed closed-won sales of $640,000 on an investment of just $18,000.)

But then came a regime change at the C-level. The new executive team decided to eliminate inside sales and sell exclusively through the channel. They wisely approved 100% MDF reimbursement to enable partners with the same automated video systems and ready-to-use campaigns their inside sales team had been using so successfully.

Up to that point, the UCC company's field marketing team had been frustrated by an embarrassing lack of professionalism and inconsistency in its partners' promotional approaches and campaigns. (Email full of typos and incorrect information was a particularly bad blotch on their brand reputation.)

By implementing an automated video platform across a wide swath of channel partners, suddenly every email from every partner rep was professional, custom-branded and personalized — and completely consistent. Many of the email campaigns also included video content, which increased prospect engagement and direct response.

Enabling channel partners with automated video was so effective that the company's transition from inside sales to channel-only sales was surprisingly seamless and did negligible damage to the company's bottom-line.

Many of that original group of partners continue to use our Automated Video Communications platform today, leveraging automated drip marketing, identifying new qualified leads, demonstrating new innovations, managing event registrations, soliciting customer feedback, and generating millions in new opportunities and closed deals. For most of these partners, it takes just one significant UCC sale to pay for a year-long automated video subscription.

10

Video production: best practices for growth hacking

B ack to your job security for a moment.

Most Channel Chiefs love the idea of using automated video for marketing and sales. But they get nervous when they need to produce the actual videos…and with good reason.

Few marketers would disagree that producing professional, customer-serving, brand-building videos is challenging. Otherwise every tech company and their channel partners would have done it already. Trying to produce professional videos without knowing the producers' secrets is like trying to build a house without a blueprint.

You'll spend a lot of time and money and wind up with a house you wouldn't even want to live in.

That said, you can't let the fear of video stop you from moving forward. It's a bad career move to sit on the sidelines with all that money and growth at stake. The longer you wait to get started, the further behind you'll be when you finally do start using video.

To help you overcome the fear and move forward with success, I've come up with five best practices for technology marketing video production. These are the vital things you must know and the rules you must follow to make sure your videos get produced in a way that reflects well on you and your company and generates growth.

These tips will save you thousands of dollars, and make you thousands more, if you follow them closely.

Best Practice #1: Provide Value

There's a big irony in producing videos today. On one hand, it's easier than ever. Everybody's walking around with a high-definition camcorder in their pocket in the form of a smartphone. It doesn't matter the brand of phone; anyone can shoot high quality visuals today. But the ready availability of phone-corders has led to a huge proliferation of videos that aren't worth watching.

Here's a fun fact: As of November 2015, approximately 500 *hours* of video were uploaded to YouTube *every minute*. *(YouTube)*

Most of those are videos that waste your time. Videos that don't have a clear purpose. Videos with poor sound. Videos that look bad and erode trust. These are what I call brand-killers, and believe me, the LAST thing you ever want to do is invest time and money to produce brand-killers.

But as the quantity of garbage-level video increases so does your opportunity to create videos that give your target audiences what they really crave—answers to their questions, deep insight into products and services, reassurance that they're making the right decisions, and real value for the time they spend watching.

So here's a complete video production philosophy summed in two words: PROVIDE VALUE. Measure everything against this standard. Ask yourself at every stage of production, *"does this provide real value?"* The answer holds the power to cut the length of your scripts in half and double viewer engagement. Because if something in your video doesn't provide value, it shouldn't make the cut.

A complete video production philosophy summed in two words: PROVIDE VALUE

Best Practice #2: Narrow Your Targets

How can you ensure your videos *really* provide value? The most effective way is through narrow targeting. As you produce any video, the easiest way to double or triple its effectiveness is to decide exactly who you're talking to and understand what they care about.

Tech vendors, manufacturers in particular, struggle to narrow down their target audiences and often pass that responsibility on to their partners. That's not surprising, because most manufacturers try to build products that work well for the largest possible horizontal swath of companies and organizations. But when it comes to marketing and selling those horizontally relevant products and services, it's time to *get vertical.*

The more you produce videos that focus on specific industries and sectors, the more successful you and your partners will be. Targeting horizontally using titles/positions, company size and geographic areas is better than no targeting at all, but it doesn't give Channel Chiefs the proven advantages of narrowing vertically. The narrower the better.

How to optimize your targets for effective vertical marketing and video production

Vertical target optimization involves discovering the ideal level of targeting and exploiting the differing needs of specific industry sectors. The purpose is to find out which product features serve each market, and the ideal terminology you need to convey benefits of each feature to each target group.

1) Create a spreadsheet for the product you'll promote in your video.

2) In the far left column, make a row-by-row list of ALL the Features your product offers, regardless of industry. For example, for a Hosted Voice offering, you might list features like Infinite Scalability, OpEx Billing, Teleworking, Presence, etc.

3) In each remaining column, add a header identifying a particular vertical sector you serve, e.g., Financial services, Hospitality, Education, Automotive, Medical/Hospital.

4) Finally, fill in all the empty boxes with the most important benefit of each feature, using words best understood and applied to each vertical sector.

To clarify, all those empty boxes will get filled with a description of the principal benefit each feature provides to a given industry sector:

- how the feature helps their specific type of business
- the problem it solves for them, and/or
- the reason they need this feature right now

You'll usually notice a pattern. Certain features offer similar benefits to multiple sectors with little or no difference in the vocabulary and terminology required to convey the benefit. Other features, however, might offer radically different benefits to a hospital than they do to an auto dealership. Those two types of businesses may use differing terms to describe their problem and how your product solves it.

You're looking for these differences. Each time you identify an important difference in the optimal communication approach, you are also identifying the benefit of producing a unique "vertical version" of the product video.

Occasionally, this exercise results in less vertical targeting than expected, for example when benefits terminology for two sectors is a near match. Other times, it results in further vertical splits, for example, when the benefits to Education as a whole are too general, and the category should ideally be split into K-12 Education and Higher Education to maximize target audience understanding and purchase motivations.

The targeting process can be laborious, but it's a powerful growth hack. Narrow vertical targeting helps you communicate how you solve a given vertical's biggest problems and serve their deepest needs. Narrow targeting gives you the luxury of communicating with more specificity and speaking the language of the viewer. This gives your video content way more authenticity and impact, simultaneously positioning your company (and its partners) as authorities with real value to offer.

Best Practice #3: Make it about THEM (not you)

Here's the single most important thing for you and your Marcom team to keep in mind when producing any video:

The question isn't "what are WE selling?" but rather, "what do THEY need?" If you've done the work of narrowing your target, then you're already on the way to making your video about them, not you.

Stop talking about your company. Instead ask your team this question: "How do we serve and provide real value to the people who are looking for, want or need what we're offering?"

If your videos embody this **spirit of service**, they'll advance and grow your brand naturally, they'll be an effective tool for your channel partners, and more sales and money will flow to you as a by-product. That's organic growth — the best kind.

Best Practice #4: Budget your videos based on projected results (not current circumstances)

Channel marketers and sales leaders often ask how much a video should cost. Before I answer that, let me pose an even better question: *What results will this video generate, and therefore, what's it worth to our company and our channel partners?* It's always smart to reverse-engineer your budgets with probing like this.

Here's a real-world example often played out at the partner level:

Imagine a potential UCC buyer does a Google search for "business phones" in one of your channel partner's local markets. The partner's business currently shows up on page four of the organic (unpaid) search results.

Page four means pretty much no one will dig deep enough to find your partner via a keyword search, so:

- they won't know the company exists,

- they won't visit the partner's website, and
- they won't do business with them.

As their vendor, you will miss that opportunity, too.

Now let's say you help subsidize the same partner's production of a custom video using MDF — perhaps a video with a common core of information that applies to multiple partners, but with a customized intro and closing sequence that's partner-specific.

Your partner posts the custom video on their own YouTube channel, embeds the video in their home page, and they spread it around their local market via automated campaigns and social media distribution. They quickly generate a few thousand views.

As you saw in the video statistics in Chapter 7, **a video on your partner's home page increases their chance of a page one Google result by a factor of 53**. Within 90 days, the partner company's site begins appearing on page one when a potential buyer searches locally for business phones.

Suddenly your partner is getting two or more hot leads per week directly from organic search. That's eight qualified leads per month. At least one of them converts into a UCC deal worth an average of $10,000. Those 12 deals a year yield top-line incremental revenue to your partner of at least $120,000 and about $48,000 in profit. You, the manufacturer-vendor, gain over $70,000 in annual sales.

Now revisit the original question: *what is the value of your partner's custom video and what should your company be willing to chip in to get it produced?*

You project a gain of over $70k in incremental annual sales revenue through that partner. Are you willing to invest just 10% of the additional sales income you're likely to earn from improved organic search placement during year one? Sounds like a bargain.

10% of $70,000 would suggest a video budget of $7,000. Coincidentally, that's about what it generally costs to produce a national-quality customized video about one-and-a-half minutes long. If you provide video marketing subsidies in the form of MDF, it reduces the net cost to you as a vendor while providing full value to the partner, so your ROI grows even more. All the pieces start to fit when you think of video marketing and production budgets with this kind of logic.

When it comes to ballpark budgets, most standard business videos — not clever high-budget ads — can be produced for about $5,000 per-finished-minute. At that price, and with most of them clocking in under 2 minutes, they're pretty much guaranteed to pay for themselves and generate positive returns within 3-6 months.

By the way, $5,000 per-finished-minute usually covers standard business videos in most of the styles that are proven to be effective:
- Concierge style (on-camera host with motion graphics)
- Animated Whiteboard (artist's hand drawing the content)
- Full Animation
- Customer Stories (on-location testimonials and case studies)

Concierge-style

Animated Whiteboard

Full Animation

Customer Stories

Common & Effective Business Video Styles

The more time you spend in the growth hacker mindset, and the more success you experience, the more your production costs will be trumped by the growth results your video content generates. Sometimes you'll want to boost your video budget to produce something unusual or extraordinary — something with obvious viral potential. If your gut says *go*, you probably should!

While a 1:1 measure of each video's success is important, a library of videos almost always has a cumulative and synergistic growth effect. They build on each other; the more high-quality video content you have for each stage of your sales funnel, the more effective your overall video growth hacking strategy is likely to be.

Some Channel Chiefs are natural bargain hunters and coupon clippers. When they hear $5000 per-finished-minute, they immediately think, *I can get it done cheaper.* Of course they can.

Some think: *I've got an iPhone and iMovie; I'll just do this myself,* or *I'll find a videographer with less experience, and supervise them more.* (Like your friend's son who's in film school.) Which leads us to…

Best Practice #5:
Hire a results-oriented visual storyteller

Very few videographers and producers are video growth hackers. So there's often a hidden cost to "saving money" on a video production.

I urge every channel chief to to seek out and hire an experienced producer with a proven record of helping clients achieve real growth — a producer whose videos tell stories at a level of quality that inherently reflects your high quality brand. And someone whose work is proven to generate consistently positive financial results. The difference in results generated by one producer (or production company) vs. another is often jaw-dropping. It's matter of money out the window vs. money in the bank.

Before signing any production contract, ask to see the producer's work *and* the financial results of how their work was used. This will weed out numerous producers and the people I fondly call "vidiots."

11

Your videos are your company

Bear in mind that every professionally produced video adds to your library and has the potential to become a strategic marketing and sales asset with a long shelf life.

Your strategic videos communicate on behalf of your company. They communicate *to* and *through* your channel — in many cases for years to come. They are a proxy, a clone of you and/or your partners, so you should be proud of them. They must convey the value you provide and tell your company's and your product's differentiating story exactly the way you want it told for maximum understanding and impact.

Strategic videos do the heavy lifting of:
- helping partners find new leads
- convincing and converting them
- saving your partners time
- lining partners' bank accounts…and yours.

When thought of this way, videos that succeed in capturing the essence of the value your company and your partners provide are a Very Big Deal. They're one key to achieving the lofty goals stated in your job description and ultimately, to achieving the career and work-life balance you want.

You, your partners, your prospects and customers all deserve excellent automated videos that represent you properly at every stage of the Buyer's Journey and Customer Lifecycle, so cutting corners is never a wise goal.

When they're done right, the videos you provide for channel use will give partners the extraordinary new freedom *not* to have to communicate everything themselves, and often *not* to have to do it in person. Partners gain essential time to work *on* their businesses, not just *in* them, as entrepreneurial expert Michael E. Gerber advocates in his book, *The E-Myth Revisited.* This freedom and objectivity is a higher form of channel enablement, and it's an important way that smart Channel Chiefs are driving consistent double-digit growth.

▶

Section 3

Automated video: faster routes to faster growth

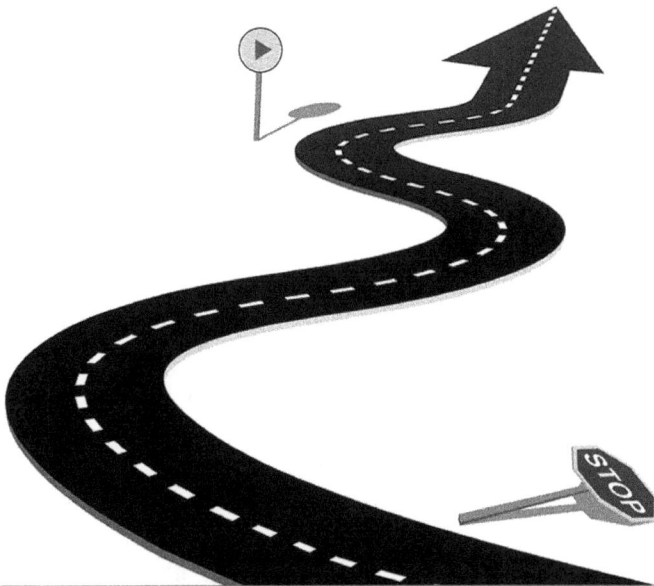

12

The role of video in the Customer Lifecycle: a faster way from A to B

L et's explore proven video strategies for tech vendors and their Value Added Resellers (VARs). Marketer Matt Heinz says, "Marketing isn't just about the top of the funnel. It doesn't stop when leads have been passed to sales." He calls marketing over the whole span of the customer relationship Full Funnel Marketing.

First you fill the funnel, then you **own the entire customer journey through ongoing video outreach**. This revolutionizes your channel strategy and generates much higher levels of success.

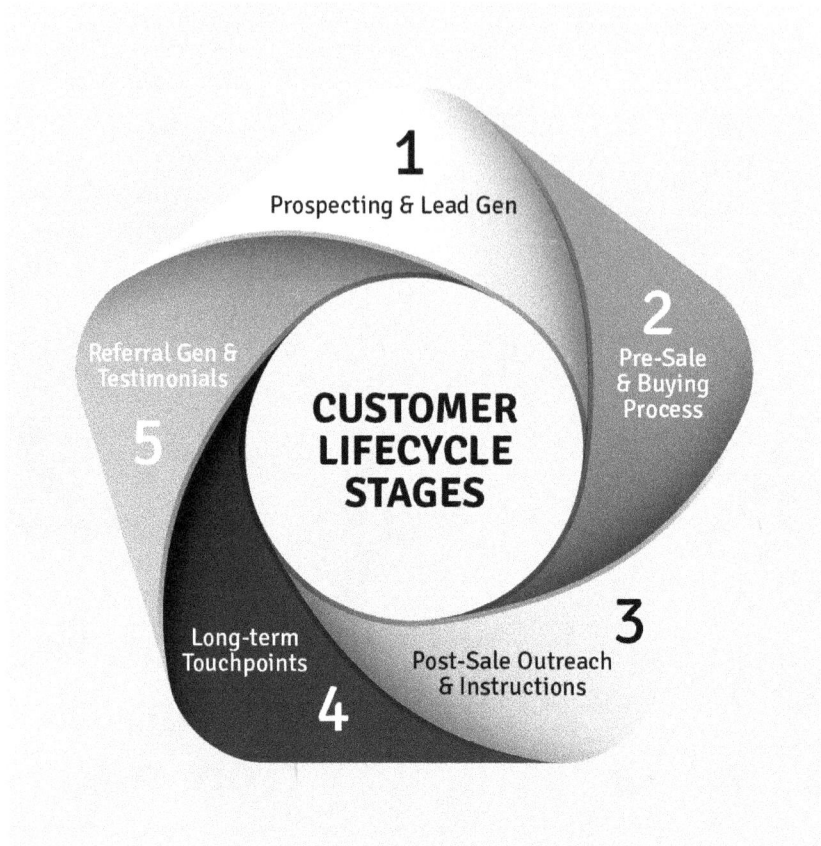

1
Prospecting & Lead Gen

2
Pre-Sale
& Buying
Process

Referral Gen &
Testimonials

**CUSTOMER
LIFECYCLE
STAGES**

5

3

Long-term
Touchpoints

Post-Sale Outreach
& Instructions

4

At Voodoo, we map out video strategies in relation to the full funnel — all **five stages** of the Customer Lifecycle, as shown above. Once a vendor company is *fully committed* to video growth hacking, these five stages provide the framework on which to build detailed production and deployment plans for video content at every point in the customer relationship.

But when just getting started with video, it's helpful to simplify things a bit more. I recommend thinking in terms of the *three primary phases* of the Customer Lifecycle: **1) Pre-sale, 2) Post-Sale** and **3) Referral Generation,**

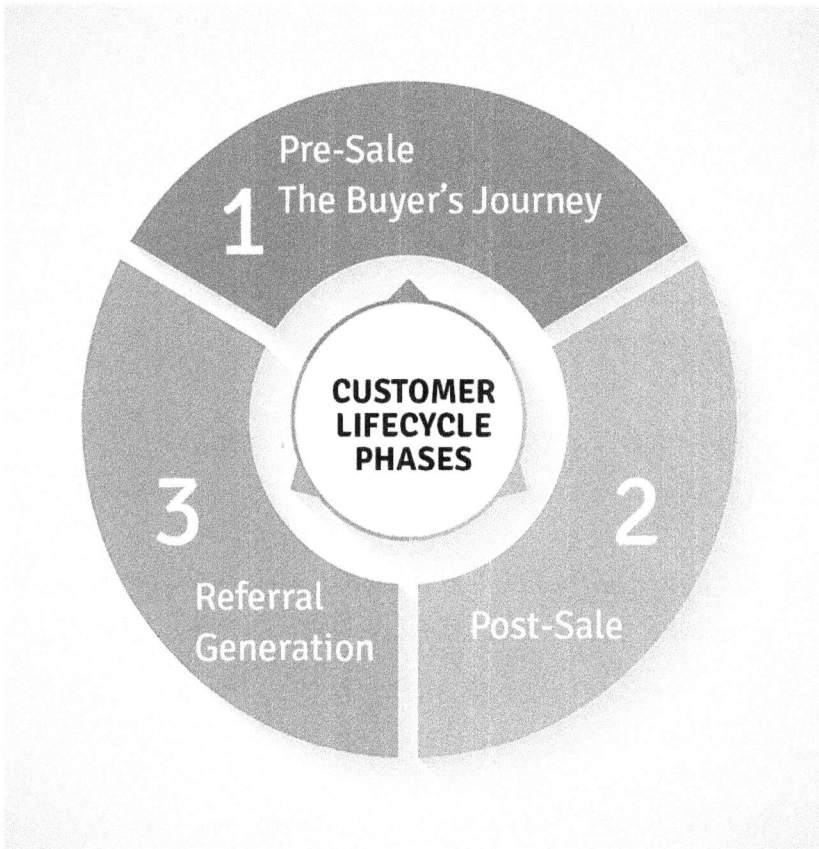

Phase 1 - Pre-Sale refers to the process of finding leads, nurturing them into prospects and converting them to paying customers. This is commonly referred to as **The Buyer's Journey**. Good news here: for most tech vendors, your company's entire video strategy is likely to pay for itself from this first stage alone.

Phase 2 - Post-Sale refers to keeping current customers informed, making sure they're happy and fully upgraded, then measuring their satisfaction. Videos used in Phase 2 do things like saying thank you to new buyers in a direct and personal way; providing essential user information and support mechanisms; anticipating customer needs;

offering add-ons and upgrades; and offering surveys to gain insight into your customers' needs and attitudes.

Phase 3 - Referral Generation involves empowering your most satisfied customers to tell others about your products and services. The most important ways to empower them are:
- to help them understand the value you provide
- to encourage them to share that value with others
- to help them communicate your value perfectly every time

Focusing first on the Pre-Sale Buyer's Journey phase and executing it effectively should be enough to transform your business and attain a significantly higher level of sales success through participating channel partners.

(Hint: Once the Pre-Sale phase is humming, you shouldn't have any trouble getting C-level support for Phases 2 and 3.)

13

The Pre-Sale Buyer's Journey & demand generation funnel

arketers often use the term demand generation to describe the goal of the Pre-Sale Buyer's Journey. Let's take a deeper look at the most efficient ways to produce targeted Pre-Sale videos to serve potential buyers as they move through the top, middle and bottom of your funnel.

Depending on the particulars of your company's sales process, your Pre-Sale videos will nurture prospects along their journey from Awareness, through Consideration to a purchase Decision.

Awareness: Top-of-Funnel (ToFu) — The prospect has identified a problem or opportunity. Use Top-of-Funnel Awareness videos to capture attention and establish your solution's relevance.

Consideration: Middle-of-Funnel (MoFu) — The prospect has named their problem or opportunity and is seeking specific solutions. Use MoFu Consideration videos to educate by giving high-level product application information and develop more interest and intent in your product.

Decision: Bottom-of-Funnel (BoFu) — The prospect understands the processes and tools needed to solve their problem or take advantage of their opportunity. Use BoFu Decision videos to provide specific information and establish functional fit, priority and potential ROI so you can differentiate your product and close more deals.

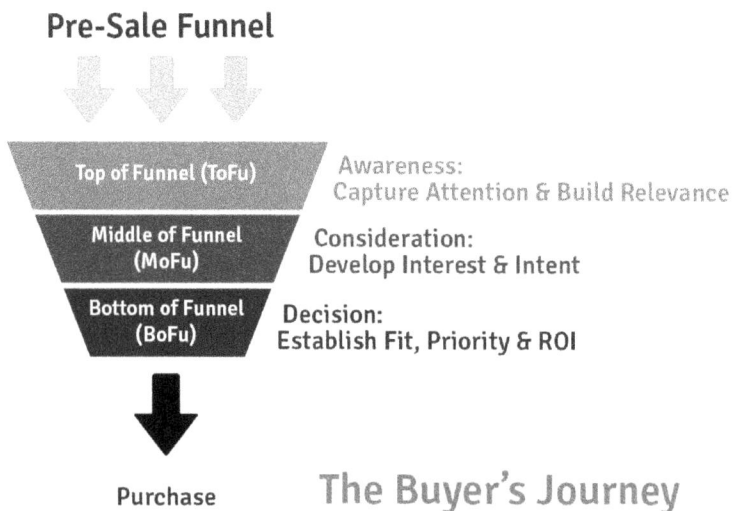

Pre-Sale Funnel

Top of Funnel (ToFu)	Awareness: Capture Attention & Build Relevance
Middle of Funnel (MoFu)	Consideration: Develop Interest & Intent
Bottom of Funnel (BoFu)	Decision: Establish Fit, Priority & ROI

Purchase

The Buyer's Journey

Top-of-Funnel (ToFu) Awareness

Top-of-Funnel (ToFu) Awareness videos are used for **attraction marketing: capturing attention and establishing relevance.** Ideally, you'll allocate a significant budget to produce awareness videos aimed at each target audience and/or vertical sector. As described earlier, if you and your partners generate significant business from sectors with differing challenges and industry lexicons, each one deserves a video version of its own.

Remember, the top of the funnel is the initial *attraction* stage. It's like walking into a party and meeting someone for the first time. Talking all about yourself is the fastest way to send the person running the other direction.

The same rule applies to your videos. Because they aim to attract new prospects, **your videos cannot be all about you.** Instead, they should identify the pain points and needs of each target group and show how your technologies can relieve their pain, solve their problems or help them realize an opportunity.

Notice that I said "your technologies," and not "your company." That's an important distinction. At this early awareness stage, the more informational and less promotional your videos are, the better. **Providing useful content as the core of your promotional strategy is what's known as *Content Marketing*.** Content is the fastest growing kind of online marketing precisely because it works so well.

Helpful content (not branded hype) is what today's buyers want from the companies and people they do business with.

So if at all possible, **resist the urge to mention specific product names or to push your brand identity** in your ToFu videos. I dare you! It may sound counter-intuitive, especially because we're all accustomed to the brand awareness mentality of television advertising. (Also, at most companies, the Marcom team generally insists on branding everything.)

But by producing minimally branded (or even non-branded) ToFu videos for your partners to use, you'll be arming them with powerful video *content* — something much more powerful and effective than video *advertising*. Based on many years of campaign statistics, it's a simple fact that **content videos are far more effective than video ads** to help your partners find qualified leads, gain trusted advisor status and start setting more sales appointments.

Does the idea of videos without your logo and product names make you nervous? It should. It's natural for a Channel Chief to want to protect their company's brand and competitive advantage.

You may be asking yourself: *How can I make sure an unbranded awareness video won't engage a new prospect only for our partner to sell a* competitive vendor's *product to the prospect?*

The truth is, you can't. But you can mitigate the downside risk so you benefit from the far greater upside potential that content marketing offers.

Start by taking a courageous, generous and long-term view: **Your partners' success is your success.** Sometimes a partner's sale of a product other than yours is simply a matter of budget and product fit at that moment for that end-user. As each partner adds sophistication, authenticity and automation to how they communicate, I guarantee you will sell more—probably far more—through that partner. Video growth hacking takes confidence and courage, but I have yet to see courageous choices go unrewarded.

Next, while they may not display your company logo or mention specific products, your **ToFu videos can still be infused with your branding standards**: company colors, fonts, photography and videography styles, etc.

You can also **leverage your product's unique benefits**. In your minimally branded or non-branded attraction and awareness videos, you will demonstrate solutions to customer pain points. Some product benefits are likely to be generic and common to your and your competitors' products. However, when a benefit or solution is unique to your technology and significantly different or better than what your competitors offer, *feature it*. Doing so will prompt deeper exploration and inquiry by the prospective buyer. And if the buyer values that benefit, your reseller *will* sell them your product.

In any case, attraction videos should be your first priority as you start Video Growth Hacking to pull more prospects into the top of the funnel. Prospect-centric video content is the fastest way for your partners to find qualified leads and have more substantive conversations earlier in their greenfield relationships.

The case for **vendor-agnostic** top-of-funnel videos

In 2015, Voodoo pulled together an advisory board of successful telecom resellers. We asked them what kind of videos they needed to improve their prospecting efforts with automated video.

What was missing from their video funnel? What videos weren't their vendor-manufacturers providing that the partners absolutely needed?

The answer was unanimous: every partner needed 'vendor-agnostic,' top-of-funnel videos to build awareness and identify qualified leads.

For them, vendor-agnostic meant the videos would include no mention of any specific manufacturer or brand. The goal was to generate demand using the partner's "non-partisan" brand before pushing any particular manufacturer or solution.

Thanks to this group's input, we began producing a series of unbranded ToFu awareness videos — animated whiteboard explainer videos covering essential benefits of technologies including VoIP, Unified Communications and Hosted Voice.

Winning the Game of Business

Lose the Chains

Legacy Island

TELE Talk - VoIP

Animated Whiteboard Videos for ToFu Prospecting

We chose whiteboard animations because Voodoo's aggregated campaign statistics had been demonstrating their rising popularity and effectiveness. Over the past two years, a growing percentage of people had been clicking-through to watch whiteboard videos.

They're also more "sticky." In A/B tests conducted by psychologist Richard Wiseman PhD, whiteboard videos (sometimes called scribe videos) were shown to produce a 15% increase in memory recall compared to talking head videos. Viewers are mesmerized by an artist's hand creating detailed drawings. The desire to see what gets drawn next makes viewers watch the videos all the way to the end.

Whiteboards are a good choice for the Attraction and Awareness stage because they're engaging, entertaining and completely non-threatening. They don't feel like a sales pitch. The best ones make prospects relax and smile—exactly the response you want at the inception of a business relationship.

We offered the new series of prospecting videos to multiple telecom resellers through their Voodoo accounts. It immediately filled a crucial gap their vendor companies had unintentionally left empty.

All partners had to do was schedule their pre-written, pre-built campaigns featuring these videos. Almost immediately after the first launch came the magic moment when hot lead notifications started to arrive, showing each sales rep exactly who was watching and who needed a follow up call to secure an appointment.

Many partners also posted their co-branded and personalized videos on Facebook, LinkedIn and Twitter. This helped them build traffic, engagement, fans, connections and followers. They could see exactly how many people clicked through to watch from each post, and they benefited from surprisingly high view rates. When any prospect in any social feed wanted to know more, the rep who posted the video received the direct response.

This prospecting program has been so popular and successful that we've now extended our production of vendor-agnostic

ToFu awareness and prospecting videos to include other tech products and categories.

The Middle and Bottom-of-Funnel

Let's take a quick look at the Consideration and Decision process and your Middle and Bottom-of-Funnel videos.

Videos in these stages should increase buyer interest and intent, and really good ones will drive action to the next stage in the buyer's journey, making it much easier for partners to close deals.

Most tech manufacturers have good-to-excellent vendor- and solution-specific videos for these purposes. Here's where **branding becomes more expected and acceptable** and less of a turn-off—as long as it's not heavy-handed.

By the way, there's no dividing line and quite a lot of crossover in the Consideration and Decision stages. Sometimes a single video may be relevant in helping a prospect both consider and decide.

Examples of MoFu Consideration videos:
- **Product Explainers**
- **How-to Videos** — solve a specific problem with your technology
- **Product Overviews and Micro Demos** — look under the hood and show products in action

- **Educational Webinars/Presentations** — long-form okay

Examples BoFu Decision videos:
- **"About us" videos** — company culture and mission
- **Customer Stories/Case Studies** — prove real-world value
- **Detailed demos/instructionals** — appease analytic types

If your company is like most tech vendor-manufacturers, your Channel or Field Marketing and corporate Marcom departments have already spent serious time and money producing MoFu and BoFu videos.

But it's often a struggle to put your videos in channel partners' hands and get them to share and leverage the videos consistently. You need tools that make it easy for partners to use video more effectively and more often. And tools that let you measure partners' video usage so you can tie it to their sales increases.

14

Beyond the purchase: Post-Sale touchpoints & Referral Generation

When you begin Video Growth Hacking, it's natural to focus solely on The Buyer's Journey, the Pre-Sale phase. Whenever possible, you'll want to arm your partners with an automated funnel to deliver videos that educate prospects and ultimately encourage them to buy. Focusing on Pre-Sale videos is the most obvious, predictably exponential way to sell more, faster, and collect your winnings.

But at risk of sounding like a huckster: *Wait! There's More!* I've worked with numerous Channel Chiefs who were surprised to find out that the later phases of the Customer Lifecycle — *after* the prospect buys — contain just as much, if not more, growth hacking potential than phase one.

As mentioned earlier, you need to do more than fill the funnel. You need to own the entire customer journey. Three reasons why:
- It costs between 5 and 12 times more to attract a new customer than to keep an existing one.
- The ROI is up to 10 times higher for investments in customer retention than new customer acquisition.
- A mere 5% increase in customer retention typically results in a 75% increase in aggregate lifetime profits.

The more competition you and your products face, the more important the post-sale customer retention and referral generation phases of the Customer Lifecycle become. That's because, according to the Gartner Group, an astounding 80 percent of your future profits are likely to come from just 20 percent of your existing customers.

Automated video is an efficient way to increase the lifetime value of customers and empower satisfied customers to become advocates so you can grow your business and fight off competition.

Case study: Using video to enhance customer satisfaction and measure it

A large manufacturer of business and consumer electronics asked us to consult with them about mounting challenges in one of their manufacturing divisions.

The company manufactures customized high-end personal electronics for a primarily B2B audience in the music industry, targeting an elite clientele of celebrities and audiophiles.

The company prides itself on providing the ultimate Customer Experience (CX). They measure customer satisfaction using the Net Promoter Score (NPS), which ranks how likely customers are to recommend the product to others. It also lets the company see how well its customer satisfaction levels compare to its competitors.

The company was growing rapidly and finding it increasingly difficult to keep each and every customer satisfied. Their big red flag was product return rates, which had recently spiked. Each return was both costly (as much as $600 in lost income) and damaging to the company's reputation.

Both Sales and Marketing knew that the high return rate wasn't caused by product defects. The root of the problem was user error. A growing number of purchasers were using the product incorrectly, but they never took responsibility— they just blamed the manufacturer.

Why was this happening? Every product was shipped with a beautiful instruction booklet—clearly written, expertly designed and expensively printed. That didn't matter, because more and more buyers just weren't taking the time to read.

Video to the rescue

Stats show that most people would prefer to watch a video than read. And remember, viewers recall 95% of what they see in a video compared to just 10% for text.

Our Video Growth Hacking doctors wrote up this simple prescription:
- Reach out to customers after the sale with a series of strategic video messages.
- Automate the videos to reach buyers at critical moments in their Customer Experience (see diagram).

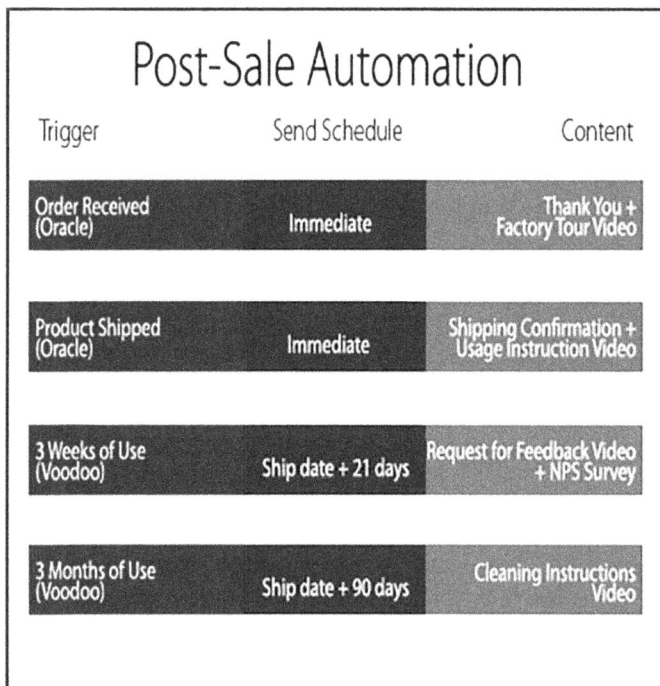

Post-Sale Automation

Trigger	Send Schedule	Content
Order Received (Oracle)	Immediate	Thank You + Factory Tour Video
Product Shipped (Oracle)	Immediate	Shipping Confirmation + Usage Instruction Video
3 Weeks of Use (Voodoo)	Ship date + 21 days	Request for Feedback Video + NPS Survey
3 Months of Use (Voodoo)	Ship date + 90 days	Cleaning Instructions Video

Post-sale videos: 3 essential touchpoints + 1 extra

Automated video was linked directly into the company's Oracle database to trigger a personalized eVideo (email + video) message, launched immediately after each order was received and processed.

Video #1 said **thank you in a unique and powerful way** and reinforced the buyer's choice by explaining the extraordinary value of the product they'd purchased. It also built excitement by giving buyers a glimpse into the factory and the custom manufacturing process.

Video #2 was triggered when the product shipped to the customer. This updated the customer with the exciting news that their product was on its way, and also provided live-action instructions about how to use it properly. In other words, **it was a video instruction manual, disguised as a product shipping update**.

Video #3 was sent 21 days after shipping, to reinforce their wise buying decision once again, to affirm that they were enjoying the product, and **to ask the customer to provide feedback via an NPS survey**.

A couple years into the program, the company identified one more problem/opportunity. Historical customer data showed the top reason customers became dissatisfied 3 months or more after buying was that the product sometimes failed due to improper care. So they added **Video #4**, sent 90 days after shipping, to **check in with the customer and offer cleaning and maintenance tips**.

Unexpected results

Everyone involved in developing this campaign believed it would work. We expected to improve the Customer Experience (CX) through strategic touchpoints after each purchase. We assumed customers would appreciate receiving consistent "personal attention," even as the company invested no staff time providing that personal service.

No one anticipated the overwhelming customer response and the domino-effect of benefits the initial trio of videos would generate. From the moment the campaign went live, the following marketing miracles occurred:

1) **Buyer's remorse was virtually eliminated.** The company stopped receiving order cancelations from buyers having second thoughts about spending so much on a personal electronic device. Customer service requests and order inquiries also decreased, saving significant soft costs.
2) **Product returns immediately dropped by 84.8%.** This was the urgent problem they needed to solve and the "video instruction manual" did the trick.
3) The company's **survey participation and Net Promoter Score immediately doubled** to +/- 80, earning their division a ranking consistent with the top five US companies. Their NPS became the highest among all

their parent company's divisions and remained there over the entire multi-year lifespan of the program. (5 years!)

This targeted, strategically triggered drip campaign generated the following cumulative Open and Click-Through Rates (CTR):

Video #1 — Thank You & Factory Tour

Open: 72.9%

CTR: 82.7% (Video Viewers)

Re-View: 72.3%

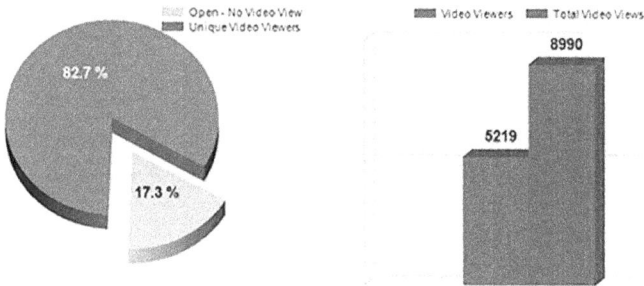

Custom Post-Sale Campaign #1 - Order Purchased

| Sent On: | 10/11/2009 6:26 PM | Status: | Sent |
| Contact List: | Custom Post-Sale Campaign Recipients | Status Date: | 8/8/2014 5:58 PM |

| 6,314 | 5,219 | 8,990 | 72.3% |
| TOTAL OPEN | VIDEO VIEWERS | TOTAL VIDEO VIEWS | RE-VIEW & PASS-ALONG RATE |

Opened: 6,314 (72.9%)

Video Viewers: 5,219

Video Click-Through Rate: 82.7%

Total Video Views: 8,990

Re-View & Pass-Along Rate: 72.3%

Video #2 — Shipping Notification & Usage Instructions

Open: 72.8%

CTR: 59.2% (Video Viewers)

Re-View: 68.6%

Custom Post-Sale Campaign #2 - Order Shipped

Sent On: **10/11/2009 6:33 PM**   Status: **Sent**

Contact List: **Custom Post-Sale Campaign Recipients**   Status Date: **1/8/2015 12:08 PM**

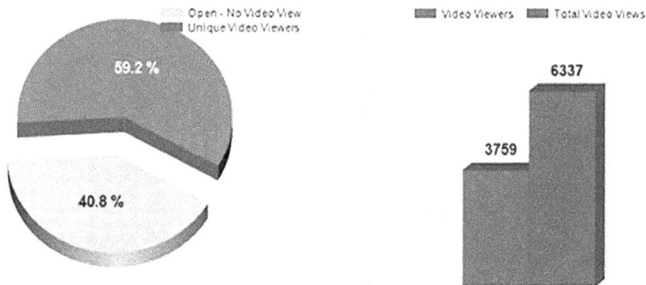

Open - No Video View
Unique Video Viewers

59.2 %

40.8 %

Video Viewers   Total Video Views

6337

3759

Click on any statistic or list item for additional detail

6,349	3,759	6,337	68.6%
TOTAL OPEN	VIDEO VIEWERS	TOTAL VIDEO VIEWS	RE-VIEW & PASS-ALONG RATE

Opened: **6,349** (72.8%)

Video Viewers: **3,759**

Video Click-Through Rate: **59.2%**

Total Video Views: **6,337**

Re-View & Pass-Along Rate: **68.6%**

Video #3 — 3-Week Check-In for Customer Feedback

Open: 65.3%

CTR: 49.2% (NPS Survey)

Re-View: 34.8%

Custom Post-Sale Campaign #3 - Order Followup

Sent On: **10/12/2009 6:33 PM**   Status: **Sent**

Contact List: **Custom Post-Sale Campaign Recipients**   Status Date: **1/22/2015 12:07 PM**

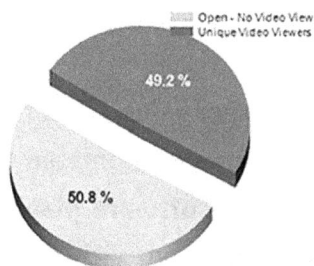

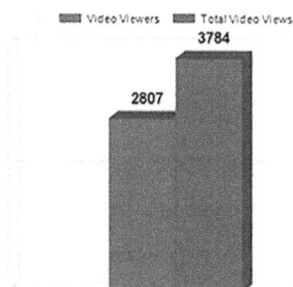

Open - No Video View
Unique Video Viewers

49.2 %

50.8 %

Video Viewers   Total Video Views

3784

2807

Click on any statistic or list item for additional detail

5,704	2,807	3,784	34.8%
TOTAL OPEN	VIDEO VIEWERS	TOTAL VIDEO VIEWS	RE-VIEW & PASS-ALONG RATE

Opened: **5,704 (65.3%)**

Video Viewers: **2,807**

Video Click-Through Rate: **49.2%**

Total Video Views: **3,784**

Re-View & Pass-Along Rate: **34.8%**

As anyone familiar with email open and click rates will tell you, this campaign commanded a crazy level of engagement and response.

Customer evangelists and bonus benefits

If the marketing miracles and extreme customer engagement weren't already enough, numerous customers spontaneously and publicly began raving about their exceptional CX in professional blogs and to friends and colleagues on social media. Customers specifically mentioned the company's innovative, helpful and "personal" eVideo messages.

While it's impossible to measure the exact value of all these benefits and positive exposure, the company estimated that **the entire cost of the automated video software platform and video production costs were amortized within three months**, due to savings both from decreases in product return costs and the value of staff time previously spent on direct customer service.

And what about the value of a Net Promoter Score of 80? Thousands of loyal customers confirming that they're eager to recommend your products? Priceless.

Section 4

Proven video strategies: turning your roadmap into a flight plan

15

Driving on autopilot: automation, co-branding & personalization

The post-sale video initiative I just described would never have been such a grand-slam without comprehensive video automation tied directly to the manufacturer's business and customer service processes and touchpoints. (The video triggering, framing, sending and tracking processes all were automated.)

To growth hack channel sales with video during all stages and phases of the Customer Lifecycle, video deployment through your VARs must also be as automated as possible. Partners are already overwhelmed, so the less they have to do and remember, the better. Otherwise sales opportunities will keep falling through the cracks.

There are **three kinds of automation** you will rely on for exponential video growth hacking:

1) **Triggering (sales process and date/time) automation** — a pre- or post-sale event triggers your video deployment system to narrowcast or broadcast video content to specific recipients

2) **Video formatting and framing automation** — your deployment system "gift-wraps" the video content, co-branding it for the partner and/or personalizing it for each individual sales rep

3) **Tracking and notification automation** — your deployment system tracks email Opens, Video Views and Shares, pdf downloads, survey responses, etc. The system also provides real-time action alerts to notify reps when they need to follow up to seize an opportunity.

When put into practice, your automated triggers should be tied to your partners' sales processes, important customer lifecycle touchpoints, promotional and/or seasonal calendars, customer satisfaction assessments, etc.

Ideally, **every video distributed should be co-branded for each partner company and personalized for each one of their sales reps.** Co-branding gets partners excited about using vendor video content in their email + video (eVideo) campaigns and social media posts.

In Chapter 17, we'll explore how segmenting your contact lists and sending eVideo campaigns from individual reps instead of a centralized company email address can yield remarkable increases in email Open and Video View rates. (Adding a photo of the rep can yield an extra 3-7% boost.)

As a video gets distributed through outbound email and social campaigns, **reps should be able to choose which real-time notifications they want or need to receive**. These "action alerts" inform reps about specific prospect and customer interactions with campaign elements. Prospects who click-through to watch videos, access other content and take surveys are often hot leads—ready to book appointments, learn more and buy soon. That's why automated tracking and notification are essential.

Ongoing fully automated video marketing processes become cumulative and synergistic. They allow your partners to deliver the *right video content* in the *right format* to the *right people* at the *right time*. I think of these processes as **potentized video marketing** — the extra-strength way to generate seemingly unlimited channel growth with surprisingly limited effort.

Eventually, you'll want to produce and deploy a complete set of strategic videos covering the full span of the **Pre-Sale Buyer's Journey** and the **Post-Sale** and **Referral Generation** phases. Leveraging videos at every stage will do a lot of otherwise difficult and repetitive work for you and your partners.

16

Deep automation: how grounded marketing vehicles take flight

L et's touch briefly on deployment tools and specific features you'll need to automate your use of video communications, and particularly the use of video to and through your channel. The right toolset eliminates friction in the partner enablement process — friction that can drag programs down and keep them grounded. Deploying video the right way will help your programs get airborne.

There's an absurd number of marketing automation tools on the market today — over 150 at last count. Most of the core channel enablement processes I'm about to share could be assembled using almost any marketing automation platform in combination with other cloud-based systems, along with plenty of custom graphic design. For example, you could combine a marketing automation system + a video hosting service + a CRM + a survey tool, then add customized design to brand the elements for each channel partner.

As a Channel Chief, you're certainly familiar with these tools. It's easy to envision how you'd piece together their varied capabilities to create a viable video automation process. But you're probably already wary of the complexity it would require.

You know the resistance that surfaces when you attempt to push any marketing process involving multiple systems onto your diverse group of channel partners. Even the tightest integration between multiple platforms requires partners to adopt all the tools required for them to launch and track campaigns successfully. I've seen vendors try this, but I also know from experience, it rarely, if ever, works like they'd hoped. (Such an understatement.)

Most partners have no interest in complicating their processes or adding to the systems they use.

Most partners already have some or all of their marketing bases covered. They have no interest in complicating their processes or adding to the number and type of systems they use. Not surprisingly, partners strongly resist partner marketing tools and systems that duplicate things they're already doing.

That being said, most partners are very hungry to leverage automated video in their marketing and sales. I'm often surprised how eagerly they'll adopt a new all-in-one solution, only if it's **centered on video.**

17

Video automation essentials: framing video content to maximize partner usage and prospect response

One key to effective channel enablement using video is to maximize the benefit your partners receive from each prospect or customer Video View.

As they share videos with contacts, each and every video should automatically be custom-branded and personalized, without needing to engage a web or graphic designer to build custom landing pages or video players.

How to maximize partner usage and prospect response

One methodology that's proven highly effective in thousands of campaigns is using an automated tool to frame each video so partners don't have to do any setup or make any modifications. In this scenario, each partner's library of professional vendor video content is automatically branded for their company and personalized for each of their reps in the frame areas surrounding the video.

The most effective configuration we've identified is for the partner company's logo and branding elements to appear at the top of the video frame, and for rep-level personalization and direct response links to appear in a footer area at the bottom of the frame.

Using the Voodoo platform, each video gets personalized for individual sales reps using one of these two footer types:

Standard footer — includes rep name, email address (live link), physical address and phone number

Digital Business Card (DBC) footer — includes all standard footer elements, plus a photo of the rep and additional branding graphics.

Both footers provide personal and direct response information, but cumulative stats confirm that including a rep's photo increases response rates by 3-7% in most campaigns. When we developed DBC automation, we had no idea such a simple concept could move the needle so dramatically on every campaign.

Partners and reps enjoy seeing their "name in lights" whenever they share videos. Professional branding and built-in direct response links generate high enthusiasm from partners and their reps who are eager to launch campaigns and post their videos on social media.

For example, when a partner rep named Jane Lucky posts one of your vendor videos on LinkedIn, she knows any and all response and inquiries generated by the video will come directly to her.

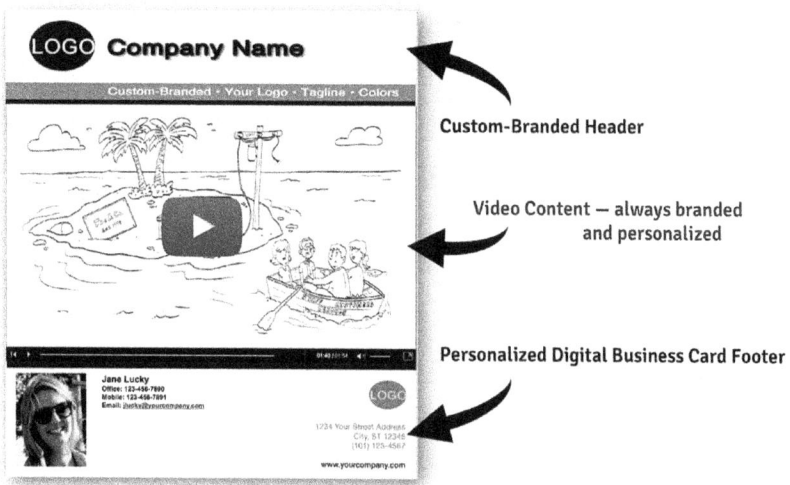

To make the video sending and sharing processes even easier, choose a video deployment platform with a mobile app so reps in the field can access and launch campaigns and share their own custom-branded and personalized videos anytime, anywhere.

Personalization: a proven multiplier

Channel Chiefs often face a battle between the convenience and manageability of mounting centralized campaigns (sent from a single email address or individual at each partner company) vs. the logistical challenge of mounting de-centralized campaigns (sent from multiple reps' email addresses at each partner company).

Often, the technological limitations of their video marketing tools lead them to choose the centralized approach. But making this choice leaves money on the table every time.

To measure the difference between centralized (corporate) and de-centralized (personal) campaigns, we set up a test campaign through a large technology distributor on behalf of a multi-location channel partner.

The core of the test was to broadcast the campaign to a director-level IT contact list. The list was divided in two. One group received the 4-stage centralized campaign from a single corporate source (company identity without individual personalization). The other group received the same 4-stage campaign de-centralized from individual representatives at the company, each using the Digital Business Card frame.

Here are the comparative results.

Centralized (corporate) campaign from company account:

900	Unique Contacts
3,600	Email Sends (4 stages with Video Link)
302	Email Opens
8.4%	Email Open Rate
19	Video Viewers

6.2%	Video Click-Through Rate
22	Total Video Views
115%	Re-View and Pass-Along Rate

De-centralized (personalized) campaign from individual sales rep accounts:

900	Unique Contacts
3,600	Email Sends (4 stages with Video Link)
824	Email Opens
22.9%	Email Open Rate
112	Video Viewers
13.6%	Video Click-Through Rate
132	Total Video Views
175%	Re-View and Pass-Along Rate

The Product Managers at the distributor and the Marketing and Sales teams at the technology partner all expected a significant difference between the corporate and personalized outreach, but no one expected the difference to be so large.

For the **personalized** campaign:
- Email Open Rate was 2.7X higher
- Video CTR was 2.2X higher
- Re-View and Pass-Along Rate was 1.5X higher—a good measure of viewer engagement

If you wonder whether you should bother to personalize your channel partner video marketing programs at the sales rep level, this example of real-world campaign performance offers a compelling incentive.

Simply by personalizing your outreach from each sales rep, you can expect an immediate doubling (or more) of your campaign Open rates and Video View CTR. This, in turn, doubles the number of hot lead notifications sales reps receive and the number of follow-up calls they'll make to set appointments.

In other words, rep-level personalization is a major Video Growth Hacking advantage.

18

The paradox of partner tiers and growth potential

E very vendor defines partner tiers in its own unique way, but usually tied to dollar sales volume. Lower tier partners are generally lower volume partners, and the middle and upper tiers account for progressively more sales and income per account.

For this reason, vendors tend to lavish a lot of attention on upper tier partners. Channel account managers spend lots of schmooze time with these big fish. Many vendors' MDF and channel enablement programs and tools will favor large partners, too.

Channel Chiefs rightly see the top tier as a hugely valuable asset. In most cases, partners in this tier are already performing well, and their sheer size demands attention and TLC. A mere 3% sales increase in one $10 million account yields $300,000 in net new income.

From an income standpoint, it's important to nurture the top tier, but make sure it's not at the expense of the lower tiers. In most cases, the big fish are larger and slower-moving, and their growth is therefore incremental, with realistic annual growth goals typically between 3-10%.

From a growth hacker's standpoint, and on a percentage basis, the middle and lower tiers — sometimes even the non-qualifying "authorized" tier — have the most explosive growth potential. It's probable that investing more into lower tier partners, and enabling their marketing and sales more effectively, will ultimately produce greater exponential growth than similar efforts with large partners.

The following chart illustrates this. Here are an actual tech vendor's qualifying partner tiers with sample growth data showing the incremental income projected from an identical average growth rate of 5% at each tier:

Top Tier	25 accounts	> $1M (avg $1.7M) @5% growth = $2.1M
Middle Tier	100 accounts	> $500k (avg $700k) @5% growth = $3.5M
Lower Tier	300 accounts	> $100k (avg $230k) @5% growth = $3.5M
Authorized	1000 accounts	< $100k (avg $30k) @5% growth = $1.5M

Note the higher incremental income amounts in the Middle

and Lower tiers, demonstrating their importance and extraordinary contributions to growth. This phenomenon is a key reason why it's often easier for Channel Chiefs to move the sales needle more dramatically at the middle and lower tiers than at the upper tier.

Imagine taking a large group of authorized partners, each of whom sold an average of $30k each last year, collectively contributing about $30 million in sales. Now give them all a simple low-cost way to increase their sales to an average of $45k each. Suddenly the lowest tier is contributing $45 million annually. On a percentage basis, that's year-over-year growth of 50%.

More and more Channel Chiefs are recognizing the phenomenal potential of their middle and lower tiers and are expanding MDF eligibility, benefits and enablement programs accordingly.

19

Small partner program adoption

Partners of various sizes and with varying degrees of marketing sophistication have very different priorities and needs when it comes to adopting a video growth hacking program.

Most vendors have one or more underperforming medium or large partners stuck at the lower tiers. But the majority of lower tier partners are smaller mom and pop resellers. For the following discussion, I'm referring to these small partners, usually with a sales team of 5 or fewer and little or no on-staff marketing support.

Small partners are *time-starved*. For them to adopt any new video-centric channel enablement solution or program, it must be radically simple and allow them to use custom-branded and personalized video with little or no learning curve. The key determinant in their decision to participate in any video marketing program you offer will be the anticipated drain on their staff time, which is always at a premium for small partners.

How much staff time will it consume to start launching partner enablement campaigns and begin receiving hot lead notifications identifying specific opportunities? If it will require more than an hour of setup and launch time, you'll get pushback and your partners will short-circuit the program adoption process. Keep setup and launch time under 30 minutes and you're likely get both their attention and a decent level of participation.

Small partners are time-starved. For them to adopt any new video-centric channel enablement solution, it must be radically simple.

Having encountered this time crunch so often, when Voodoo's engineering team began developing a "lite" partner enablement tool targeted to small partners, the goal was to create a foolproof app partners could use to launch their first eVideo campaign in 10 minutes or less. If they knew they'd only have to invest 10 minutes to start adding new leads to their pipeline, they'd have no excuse not to try it, if only out of curiosity.

We gave the lite tool a simple descriptive name: the *eVideo Launcher*. By the time it went live in 2013, we had trimmed initial campaign launch time down to just 5 minutes.

The first two vendors that offered this tool to their smaller partners chose to provide a 50% MDF subsidy. The plan worked. Both vendors experienced fast-rising partner adoption with no burden on their own Channel or Field Marketing staff to provide campaign launch assistance.

The *eVideo Launcher* soon proved its merits as a foolproof do-it-yourself video marketing tool, and the first group of partners was immediately able to launch co-branded personalized video campaigns to their prospect and customer lists. Within minutes, they were receiving Video View notifications, helping them zero in on interested prospects worthy of their time and attention.

▶

20

Mid-sized partner program adoption

Mid-sized partners also want more time...*preferably at the beach!* They want **marketing and sales efficiency: to cut time off their workday while selling more**.

This groups gets excited by a fully automated video growth hacking solution — one that makes video do a lot of their repetitive prospecting and educating. They want to connect video to their sales cycle and business triggers so they can set it and forget it.

Some of the most effective mechanisms for this are:
- adding capture forms to their websites to increase lead capture and conversions

- launching one-off campaigns to large groups of new prospects and vertically targeted lists
- leveraging automated drip campaigns to nurture qualified leads and current customers
- using a mobile app to launch quick-sends to new contacts and small numbers of specific contacts on the fly
- automating contract expiration communications and renewals (e.g., software assurance, managed services)
- sending customer feedback surveys and segmenting respondents into *detractors* who need love and attention and *promoters* who are ready to advocate for you and your products
- automating referral generation programs among your promoters

---

Mid-sized partners want to connect video to their sales cycle and business triggers so they can set it and forget it.

When putting together a video marketing enablement program to serve your mid-sized partners, **make sure that any automated video system comes with a consulting package to help offset any lack of marketing staff or expertise at the partner level.** Consulting services are often essential to ensure each partner gets setup properly:

- to quickly begin launching the campaigns and funnels needed to grow sales
- to make steady progress toward automating repetitive marketing, communications and biz ops functions.

I've been engaged in a nearly decade of real-world R&D with partners at all levels, and mid-sized partners have the most widely varying video deployment needs. Over time, our team decided to offer three distinct levels of Automated Video Communications and consulting packages in order to serve every mid-sized partner as effectively as possible.

We labeled these complete platform + consulting packages *Business Builder Systems*. All three levels offer access to the complete feature list of effective mechanisms listed above, but each system type is optimized for:

- the partner's internal sales hierarchy
- the number of reps on their sales team
- the number of contacts in their greenfield and customer lists
- their marketing budget and available MDF support

21

Large partner program adoption

L arge partners always want to sell more, but prefer to do it *without moving a muscle*. Most of the major players understand and appreciate the value of high quality video content. They want videos co-branded for their company, localized to each of their branch locations, and personalized for every sales rep. At the same time, **they'd rather not have to implement any change or go outside their comfort zone at all**.

Any video-centric partner enablement tools you offer to large partners must therefore be compatible with their existing communications tools and marketing automation platforms.

Perhaps surprisingly, some large partners have requested MDF from their vendors for complete *Business Builder* accounts. These partners wanted to make video a centerpiece of their sales processes and to fill gaps in their existing marketing technology. (We've enabled and trained sales teams at some of the country's largest resellers.)

Large partners want content that's customized for their branch locations and sales reps. But they don't want to go outside their comfort zone.

In other cases, though, we've enabled large partners using simple **custom-branded and personalized video libraries**. These libraries are sets of links allowing the partner's own marketing team to benefit from custom-formatted videos, branded for the partner and personalized for each rep.

Video link libraries give a large partner's marketing team the ability to embed customized videos into inbound, outbound and social media programs *on behalf of each branch office and each rep*, without needing a graphic designer to create tens (or even hundreds) of unique video pages or frames.

22

The Video Growth Hacker's
Flight Plan

For many tech vendors and their channel partners, Automated Video Communications are an overlooked (or avoided) piece of the marketing puzzle.

But based on reams of data from thousands of campaigns, it's well-proven that **strategic video** — when launched and potentized through a comprehensive automation, co-branding, personalization and tracking platform — is a remarkably fast and easy way to growth hack channel marketing and sales. Some vendors already understand this and provide 100% MDF coverage or high-percentage subsidies for video channel enablement.

As Voodoo's platform evolves, we work to increase potency and reduce friction in each automated process, with these goals in mind:

1) **Simplify channel enablement for channel chiefs** — make video marketing easier to deploy, more effective and measurable
2) **Provide maximum sales growth for channel partners** — the highest possible ROI from the vendor's video program with the least commitment of time and little or no learning curve.

When your video channel enablement program is fully operational and optimized, it will consistently and automatically reach out on behalf of your partners and their reps. It will make your vendor or distributor business, and your partners' businesses, look great in the process. **It will consistently deliver the *right video content* in the *right format* to the *right people* at the *right time*** — a guaranteed way to build your brand and sell more with less effort.

As a Channel Chief, strategic automated video holds the key to greater job security and a better work-life balance for you — and it offers similar benefits to each channel partner you enable.

I hope you feel inspired to allocate the budget to launch or expand your video marketing efforts *now*. You'll be surprised how much easier it is to get your partner marketing vehicles and programs off the ground when you're committed to Video Growth Hacking.

▶ ▶ ▶

References

The Twelve Sales Metrics that Matter Most, Steve W. Martin, Harvard Business Review, December 9, 2013
https://hbr.org/2013/12/new-insight-into-key-sales-metrics/

Growth Hacking, Wikipedia, https://en.wikipedia.org/wiki/Growth_hacking

What is Growth Hacking? by Neil Patel and Bronson Taylor, Quicksprout
https://www.quicksprout.com/the-definitive-guide-to-growth-hacking-chapter-1/

3 Video Trands to Watch by Armando Roggio, Practical eCommerce
http://www.practicalecommerce.com/articles/3840-3-Video-Trends-to-Watch-in-2013

Easiest Way to Rank? Through Video. by Cliff Karklin, Fathom
http://www.fathomdelivers.com/blog/video/videos-seo-more-likely-to-rank/

Video Content Marketing: 4 Elements of an Effective Strategy by Rob Ciampa, Content Marketing Institute
http://contentmarketinginstitute.com/2013/03/video-content-marketing-effective-strategy/

Managing Content Marketing by Robert Rose and Joe Pulizzi, CMI Books

Linchpin: Are You Indispensible? by Seth Godin, Portfolio (Penguin)

19 Reasons You Should Use Visual Content in Your Marketing [Data] by Amanda Sibley, Hubspot Marketing Blog
http://blog.hubspot.com/blog/tabid/6307/bid/33423/19-Reasons-You-Should-Include-Visual-Content-in-Your-Marketing-Data.aspx#sm.0000btf5cqi36fsbxbo22a32wh168

Harnessing the Power of Stories by Jennifer Aaker, Stanford University
https://womensleadership.stanford.edu/stories

Marketing with Video; What's Your Story? Media Masters blog
http://www.mymediamasters.com/why-video.html

Online Publishers Association, now dba Digital Content Next
https://digitalcontentnext.org/

5 Reasons Video MUST Be Part of Your 2016 Marketing Budget [Infographic] by Eric Hinson, Vidyard
https://www.vidyard.com/blog/5-reasons-video-must-2016-marketing-budget/

GetResponse Study Shows Video Emails Increase Click-through Rates by 96 Percent, Implix/GetResponse
http://www.prnewswire.com/news-releases/getresponse-study-shows-video-emails-increase-click-through-rates-by-96-percent-78406237.html

The E-Myth Revisited: Why Most Small Businesses Don't Work and What to Do About It by Michael E. Gerber, HarperCollins

Customer Retention Should Outweigh Customer Acquisition by Jerry Jao, CMO
http://www.cmo.com/articles/2013/7/18/customer_retention.html

The Economics of E-Loyalty by Eric Reichheld and Phil Schefter, Harvard Business School, Working Knowledge
http://hbswk.hbs.edu/archive/1590.html

Full Funnel Marketing 101, Antares Advisors and Matt Heinz
http://www.antaresadvisorsgroup.com/our-thoughts/full-funnel-marketing-101

Psychology behind whiteboard videos—how they increase learning 15% , Sparkol
http://www.sparkol.com/engage/how-scribe-videos-increase-your-students-learning-by-15/

About the Author

Robert Cassard

Award-winning Writer-Producer-Director,
Video Growth Hacker & Content Strategist

Robert Cassard has written, produced and directed hundreds of corporate, commercial, educational and documentary films and videos. As a principal in multiple advertising, PR, video production and automation firms since 1987, Cassard has helped emerging and established companies grow rapidly and increase their business valuation using both viral and traditional marketing techniques.

His video growth hacking and content marketing strategies have generated fast growth and hundreds of millions in incremental sales for large organizations including *Avnet, GM, Herman Miller, Hewlett Packard Enterprise, Logitech, Make-a-Wish Foundation, Mitel, Sprint* and *Touchstone Pictures,* along with many small and mid-sized businesses and non-profits.

With partner Rick Davis, Cassard was an early pioneer in video-enhanced strategic navigation for websites. In 2007, Cassard and Davis founded *Voodoo Viral Marketing Systems*, a cloud-based software platform to automate, co-brand and personalize video communications.

Cassard has been recognized with numerous Addy and Telly Awards, Summit International Creative Awards, a Golden Eagle, and the nation's highest PR honor, the Silver Anvil Award from the Public Relations Society of America.

He is the proud father of three creative children and is a life-long singer-songwriter who performs in an alt-folk duo with his wife Bara called *Cosmic Spin.*

Author's Note:

I welcome readers to contact me to discuss how to apply the general concepts in this book to your specific challenges, opportunities and budgets. My team and I can help map video strategies, budgets and MDF programs to Video Growth Hack all five customer lifecycle stages for you and your partners. We can also help you identify the best video production resources for your situation.

email:	rcassard@voodooviral.com
	robert@videogrowthhacker.com
twitter:	@rjwcassard
web:	www.VoodooViral.com
	www.VideoGrowthHacker.com

Publisher's Note:

Business Success Press hopes you've enjoyed this book, found it valuable and will tell your colleagues about it. By special arrangement with *Voodoo Viral Marketing Systems*, anyone who reviews this book, either in a blog, online review site, Amazon.com or a public social media post will be eligible for a free confidential *Video Growth Hacking Assessment* to evaluate your current channel program and video assets. Simply send a link, photo or screen shot of your review to: team@voodooviral.com. Thank you!

#videogrowthhacking

Have Robert Cassard, the Video Growth Hacker, speak at your next event.

If you are looking for a dynamic and relevant speaker to provide breakthrough value to a business audience, Robert Cassard is an ideal choice.

Cassard earned his reputation as The Video Growth Hacker from years of helping business people use strategic video marketing to generate fast and consistent growth. He imparts the energy, wisdom and insight and from three decades as a marketing strategist and award-winning video writer-producer-director.

Cassard's entertaining talks are full of tales from the trenches, video examples, audience participation, and plenty of humor. He shares concrete ways to use automated video to achieve record-setting sales, customer satisfaction and customer referrals, along with advice about using video to improve work-life balance.

Cassard is available for keynote presentations, half-day and full-day seminars and panel discussions. He frequently shares his expertise at business schools, trade shows, marketing conferences, and business and company events in the US and internationally.

**Visit www.VideoGrowthHacker.com
for more information and to book your date.**

www.ingramcontent.com/pod-product-compliance
Lightning Source LLC
Chambersburg PA
CBHW060610200326
41521CB00007B/726